EDGAR CAYCE'S Self-Healing Tips

By Laurel Steinhice

The LightSource Group

lightsourcegroup.com

ISBN: 978-09801688-2-2

Revised Second Edition

Printed in The United States of America

Illustrations from the 1993 Edition are the original work of artist and publisher David Wilson of Lorien House, Black Mountain, North Carolina, and were prepared specifically for the production of "Self-Healing Tips."

Updated cover designs, layout and production for the second edition are by Thom W. King, KingAuthor Productions, Nashville, Tennessee.

The LightSource Group

lightsourcegroup.com

CONTENTS

01

INTRODUCTIONS AND COMMENTARIES FOR THE SECOND EDITION

Although he didn't like to be called a "psychic", the late great Edgar Cayce (1877 – 1945) was undisputedly the most prominent seer, spirit communicator and teacher of natural healing of modern times. As he "slept" in a deep trance state, spirit guides spoke through him in a decades-long series of conversations with Edgar's earthly companions, called "handlers", to reveal a vast body of knowledge that was typically beyond the reach and understanding of ordinary humans ... including Cayce himself. We are fortunate that these revelations from a higher reality were duly noted and recorded, to come into the care of the Association for Research and Enlightenment ... and to contribute significantly to beneficial natural healing practices in our society.

In his present role as elder statesman of what is sometimes called the New Age or New Spirituality movement, the highly-evolved Cayce persona now shows us the other side of the spirit-communication coin. He speaks through several channels – including me! – and shares insight and information with us that helps us to know ourselves, to heal ourselves, and to move forward along the path of enlightenment.

I've been working directly with Edgar Cayce for more than 20 years, and we work well together. I feel we know each other well, and there is a family fondness. Yet even now, from day to day as he speaks through me, he never ceases to amaze me with far-out new ideas; new visions; new self-healing skills that are actually *do-able* – and teachable, as well. Yet is also true that *yesterday's* bold new concepts, such as those given here in "Tips" have shown remarkable staying-power. In my experience, they have proven to be valid. I've used them. I've taught them. For some of us, they have become integrated into our lives in ways that directly benefit not only our spiritual growth and self-exploration adventures of realization, but also our everyday ordinary pathways.

The content of this book was first published by Lorien House in 1993 as "Edgar Cayce's Self-Healing Tips for the 90s". Edgar was given author's credit, and I was listed as the channel through whom he wrote. While that is indeed a genuine reflection of the relationship between us, in part, it's also true that I am deeply integrated into the LightSource Group (the successor to our earlier Crystal Circle), and since 'we're all One', in any case, I'm certainly a co-author of the work of our group. As the active *incarnate* co-author – the one who sits in front of the computer to enter our texts, and the one who tackles the mundane task of seeing it copyrighted, published and distributed, it is appropriate – and convenient! - for me to hold the title of "author" of this material, for practical purposes.

Edgar Cayce and I, along with the vast number of other distinguished Guides of The LightSource Group, have more books to bring you in the near future. Watch for us! It is our delight to bring through information and energies that can enLighten and enrich human lives ... and the life of planet Earth...

Laurel Steinhice,
Channel of Universal Light,
The LightSource Group
Nashville, Tennessee, October, 2009.

1

Introduction

All health is self-chosen. By right of free will, every individual Be-ing of the Universe has the right to choose that state of balanced body-mind-spirit wellness, completion, and fulfillment called "good health." Good health is the natural condition toward which all Be-ings grow and flow.

All healing is "self"-healing. The journey from imbalance and dis-ease to balanced wellness is an intensely personal one. Nobody can impose healing on someone else from the outside, by force of will. One must choose to be healed and allow self-healing energies to flow.

By right of interactive free will, every collective consciousness unit of Be-ing of the Universe also has the right to manifest self-chosen *group* health. These range from the simplest couple bonding or family unit to complex ethnic, local, tribal, national, international, affinity group, interspecies, global, galactic or Universal societies.

All healing is earth-healing. The concept of balanced wellness includes microcosm (the individual), macrocosm (the Universe), and everything in between. Every individual is an interactive part of the whole, and the individual earth Be-ing's path toward balanced wellness is a direct reflection of the developmental issues and lifepath of the Earthplanet which is your present home. Personal health is very much an integrated interactive part of Earthplanet and Universal health.

A Personal Note from Edgar Cayce

When I was Edgar Cayce, called "The Sleeping Prophet", I served as the physical instrument through which information was transmitted from spiritplane, directed by Spirit, to earthplane. By far the greater portion of this information dealt specifically with health-related matters.

I know now, even more fully than I knew then, that my chosen path is one of service. I believed then, as I believe now, that the greatest service I can render to my God and to my fellow Be-ing is to assist in bringing forth information that will stimulate and support individual, interpersonal, planetary and Universal self-healing. I am personally committed to that path.

Now instead of being the channel through whose voice information is given, I participate in giving information through the voices and hands of others. I work through and with other channels, in addition to the one through whom this set of messages is being given.

The Crystal Circle is a name we have chosen to designate our crossplane communications group. The Circle is the successor to the undefined group energy known only as Spirit, which spoke through me when I was in the Cayce incarnation. Many of the same individual Be-ings who were with me then are still active in the Circle.

The channel, Laurel, is our primary trans-channel. We maintain a significant level of communication with no fewer than 150 channels, worldwide. There is a need for many channels, in these challenging times! We have great affection and respect for each of them.

Laurel stands in special relationship to us - and to me - for a number of strong reasons. She has been carefully prepared for her present role through an infinite series of lifetimes on this planet and its spiritual predecessors as well. We have shared much, and she is greatly loved. I am the prime speaker through her because my personal vibration is the most closely matched to hers. We are deeply interconnected: we are One.

On a pragmatic level, she is also the strongest and clearest channel we know. No channel is 100% perfect; there is always room for error. The same is true for any guide or set of guides. It is to her credit (and greatly contributes to the accuracy and ease of our work!) that Laurel knows this, and does not declare herself - or us - to be infallible.

It is well that you should know this: the reader cannot rely on unfailing accuracy of information from **any** source. Each piece of information must be tested and evaluated in the Light of one's own knowing, from within. That which has value for one reader may not be appropriate for the next. For every person, the Light within is the only true authority.

In this document, Edgar Cayce speaks for The Crystal Circle. Thank you for allowing us to share information, insight, ideas and energy with you.

4

A Channel's Eye View from Laurel Steinhice

It's an honor and a delight to serve as trans-channel for Edgar Cayce and The Crystal Circle. I love my work! It's fresh and new - and challenging - every day!

I started in spirit communication when I was 12 years old, and have maintained an off-and-on contact with various guides for over 40 years. I've done a lot of living in those years. Sometimes conversation with discarnate spirits was a strong and pressing interest for me; sometimes I was focused on other things and gave it only minimal time and attention.

It was just after my husband's death-crossing transition in 1977 that I entered into a new crossplane contact phase. Bill's presence as my personal guide brought me a new level of *trust* in the channeling process. At that point most of my communication was still through automatic writing.

Over the years I had consistently shied away from becoming a professional channel, not wanting the combination of opportunity for error and probable notoriety I feared that might bring. Then in 1985 when Bill told me about a new project, one he said I had already agreed to be a part of, it felt right to me.

My late husband, Bill, was the first discarnate entity to come through me in direct voice channeling. The next was Arthur Ford.

When Bill and Arthur told me Edgar Cayce wanted to speak through me, I was bowled over. Wow! Edgar Cayce! I thought Cayce would come in for something akin to a special guest appearance; say a few words and then ride off into the metaphysical sunset leaving me looking wistfully after him like the tow-headed little boy in "Shane."

"Goodbye, Mr. Cayce ... goodbye, Mr. Cayce ..." I could just see myself in the role, watching him drift away. I would have felt honored, ever after.

I *do* feel honored ever after, but Edgar has yet to ride off into the sunset. He first came in and spoke through me on July 30, 1988, and has stayed to continue speaking through me ever since.

Edgar Cayce has opened doors for me; as a channel through whom he speaks I've been plunged headlong into topics and explorations and worlds I never knew existed. I love it! And I respect it: the information he has given through me has consistently impressed me with its quality and continuity.

Channeling Edgar Cayce has given me a chance to feel I know him personally. The channel/guide relationship is a uniquely intimate one I have come to cherish. Edgar is wonderful! And his tenets of faith, principles and philosophies are highly compatible with my own.

I agree with Edgar that no channel - or guide - is 100 percent clear, 100 percent of the time. There are no guarantees. Apart from the proof that comes from each of us, from within, I can't prove to you that our channeled information is correct or even that I'm actually channeling Edgar Cayce.

The only guarantee I can give is that **I** believe it's really Edgar Cayce. I'm convinced that he and the others who speak through me are actually, in fact, who they say they are. I also know, through my experience during four years of a full-time career as their trans-channel, that Edgar Cayce and The Crystal Circle have been remarkably consistent in giving high-level veridical information through me and through several other channels of my acquaintance. The positive impact on my life has been enormous.

Those who hear our channeling and read our channeled publications must decide for themselves. Is it really Edgar Cayce? Is the information valid?

Look to your own heart, and read the answer by the Light from within. As for me, I look forward to many more years of exciting and enlightening communication with Edgar and The Circle.

Chapter 1

NEW OPPORTUNITIES FOR SELF-HEALING

Planet earth is coming of age. This finite fragile globe and all lifeforms on it are in the process of *maturing.*

For eons now, the earth's vibrational frequency has been that of a **third dimensional planet.** When the present planetary transition (which is already well under way) has been completed, the earth's vibrational frequency will be that of a **fourth dimensional planet.** Third and fourth dimensional vibrational frequencies are both ***realities.*** There are some conditions of existence common to both these two realities, and there are also some differences between them.

Though the idea of moving into a new planetary and personal vibrational reality makes you feel something new is coming, something you've never experienced before, that's only partly true. It's only the *planet's* transition to new vibrational frequency, as a whole, that is new and dramatic. For you have experienced the fourth dimension many times before, during your sojourns on spirit planes, between incarnations.

In the historical past, how has one moved from third dimensional reality into fourth dimensional reality? By "dying."

Common practice has been for individuals to end an incarnation by undergoing the death crossing transition, at which time the physical body is sloughed off and the mind-and-spirit portion of the self, or "soul", has awakened on spirit plane, in fourth dimensional reality.

Because the whole planet is shifting to a new vibrational frequency, it is no longer necessary to "die" for an individual to move from third dimensional reality to fourth. One can adjust the vibrational frequency *while fully incarnate,* so as to move directly into fourth dimensional reality and yet maintain full continuous function on third dimensional levels as well.

You are living at a time when death is becoming an

option, rather than an unavoidable necessity. This is one of several foundations of understanding which provide the new opportunity for self-healing.

Death is still a valid option. There will be many who choose to "die". They will leave the body behind, rather than adjusting vibrational frequency so as to maintain its physical integrity during dimensional transition (whether personal, planetary or both). Those who choose the death crossing transition should not be made to feel inferior; there are many excellent reasons for choosing death.

It is important, however, to recognize the element of *choice* and let people know what a full range of options they have.

Many of you already sense instinctively that you don't have to die. You feel quite unthreatened by the idea of death. You know you can take it or leave it; you have received direct inner guidance that affirms the principle of ascension or transcendence (non-death).

Many of you are already well on the way to having manifested functional fourth dimensional vibrational frequency in your own bodies, and others are experiencing a certain confusion due to constantly swinging back and forth from third to fourth. You are standing between dimensions like the man with one foot on the dock and another on the boat, wondering when you'll lose your balance and fall into the lake!

Despite your bewilderment, clarity comes with every passing day. It gets easier to keep your balance, and suddenly people you hardly know are coming to you instinctively, looking for answers; seeking help, speaking of their own need for affirmation on the pathway of spiritual growth.

Your sensitivity to the pain of others, to the needs of nonhuman creatures and to the pitiful plight of the planet itself is rising. You care more, and you feel a need to serve others. You are increasingly aware of how much you are a part of the Universe, and Universal Light.

You are - women and men alike - becoming aware of the Goddess-energy within you; the healing LovePower which has long been associated with mothering, nurturing, care-giving roles. You are a part of that which is sometimes called the rising Christconsciousness, or Lightconsciousness. It is also called MotherLight. On the one hand you are more saddened and frustrated by the ills of society and the planet around you, and on the other hand you are becoming at peace.

These are a few of the hallmarks of someone who is in the process of manifesting fourth dimensional vibrational frequency.

Many persons have made the higher-self decision to choose non-death transition (ascension; transcendence).

You are raising personal vibrational frequency into fourth dimensional reality *now*, as a part of the wave of shifting frequency which will greatly assist the transition of the planet as a whole. There are as many variations on this series of personal adjustments is as there are individuals. It is a *personal* adjustment, defined and implemented on an individual basis by individual choices. Yet there are patterns of experience - trends - that can be clearly identified as common to a great many personal paths.

There is a quest for enlightenment, a need to understand one's life and purpose; a yearning for Oneness with the Universe; the reassurance that as individuals you are in tune with the Universe and its multifaceted manifestations of purpose of Divine Will. You feel a need to understand your role as part of the Universal; you need to know where and how you fit into the big picture.

And you need to *feel* the Oneness; the connective spiritual energy. You are experiencing a mental and spiritual growth spurt, a desire for renewal and connection. This is part of your healing.

There is a quest for personal wellness - a "fitness craze" - which prompts you to consider the condition of your physical bodies and how these can be improved. You are diet-conscious and concerned about food additives and other environmental contaminants. You are concerned about clean air and clean water not only for yourself, but for generations to come - for the health of the planet and its future inhabitants. You are growing more committed to healing that which is out of balance in your physical being, and to wholistic and/or metaphysical healing techniques. You are seeking wellness, through self-healing.

You are following the promptings of your higher self in seeking balanced wellness of body, mind and spirit. You do this instinctively, knowing it will improve the quality of your personal lives and the quality of collective planetary here-and--now reality. You do this knowing it will improve the quality of *future* reality, both personal and planetary.

In your seeking a healthy, balanced wellness of body, mind and spirit you are also raising your vibrational frequency. **You are preparing for transcendence/ascension; you are moving into the fourth dimension.**

Earth's historic timeline (and major segments of its prehistoric timeline) have been, on the whole, third dimensional. There have been individuals in the past who have personally manifested fourth and higher dimensional vibrational frequencies. Some were/are entities from other parts of the Universe, other dimensions. Some were/are ascended Masters, Avatars, teachers, enlightened Ones, personified aspects of the Universal.

Whether they achieved heightened vibrational frequency through a series of growth incarnations and "graduated" from "schoolhouse Earth" or came here from afar as members of planetary troubleshooter teams, they were/are the spiritually gifted, the authority figures and *leaders* of earthplane development. From incarnate earthplane perspective, they were exceptions to the rules. Their ways and abilities were beyond the scope of ordinary mortal experience.

They told you that someday you, too, would be like them. That whatever miracles they wrought you would also bring to pass, and more beyond! They postulated - and promised - that you, too, would achieve a new dimension of reality.

Their prophecies and promises are in the process of coming to pass even now, in your present incarnated lifetimes.

Universal access to the transcendence/ascension option is unique to the present age of transition. Never before on the earth planet has there been the opportunity, available to all - not just a few - to move directly into fourth dimensional reality without sloughing off the physical body.

This is the **NEW** opportunity for self-healing.

Chapter 2

GETTING A HANDLE ON THE SELF-HEALING PROCESS

First, slough off the old fears and perceptions that lead you to accept limitation as a way of life. Do not ask yourself, "If I could heal myself, why didn't I do it ten years ago, or last year, or six months ago?" This is not productive thinking. It sets up barriers.

Raise your level of expectation! This is the first step toward full self-healing. Propel yourself forward from *then*-thinking into *now*-thinking! In the past, the opportunity wasn't there at this new level. This is a truly NEW chance to heal yourself, and to assist others with their self-healing paths.

Now it doesn't take a great leap of faith to reverse the course of body-ravaging diseases. It only takes a small step, a wanting to be healed and a willingness to implement that decision by taking action.

With an awareness of the new level of opportunity for self-healing, remember also that healing is a balance of energies: body, mind and spirit. Healing of the body is not the sole goal - sometimes healing comes with the death crossing transition - but the full and complete healing of the body **is** an option, no matter what the present condition of that body may be.

Secondly, **approach your commitment to self-healing and fuller self-realization through a balanced approach which incorporates instinct, intuition, and intellect.** It is not unspiritual or anti-intuitive to think and act in an organized, orderly manner. How sad that some people seem to think so! Use your head! To follow one's heart need not imply an automatic rejection of one's brain and better judgment. Heart and mind should be a team, not adversaries.

Make a realistic evaluation of your own needs. Identify the aspects of your life and health that are out of balance, and find out what self-healing support resources are available to you. See what your community and your society have to offer that may be helpful, and **then follow your own inner guidance in choosing the right resources for *you*,** at any given point in your life and growthpath.

There are an ever-growing number of self-healing support resources. It makes sense to familiarize yourself with a variety of tools, techniques and philosophies on your quest for personal balance and excellence. Sample those which appeal to you and focus on the tools, techniques and philosophies (See footnote 1, in the Appendix) that meet your needs at any given time. Be open to new ideas ... and be a smart shopper!

Level of Need

There are three levels of healing need: acute, chronic, and wellness.

Acute need for healing relates to urgency. These are conditions which must be swiftly dealt with to bring immediate symptomatic relief. If not dealt with promptly they will worsen and cause further injury and/or precipitate the death crossing experience.

Acute need for healing is common in virtually *all* modern earthplane societies, and the high-technology healthcare system through which acute needs are usually addressed is proving painfully unequal to the challenge in a great and growing number of instances.

Chronic needs relate to long-standing health problems which are controllable to some degree but resistant to full and final resolution. Many persons who have "learned to live with" chronic health problems (including those conditions which are disabling or severely limiting) are now in the process of taking a fresh look at their health needs with a view toward seeking self-healing at higher levels of effectiveness.

Wellness is a term which has recently come into widespread use, indicating an improved and enhanced overall state of personal health. Everyone incarnate on planet Earth at this time has been and is constantly exposed to environmental contaminants, stress and other causes which contribute to the manifestation of less than ideal levels of personal physical, mental and spiritual health. Everyone can use some fine-tuning; everyone has a need for some level of healing.

Everyone has also accumulated a vast personal collection of *learned situational responses* during the present incarnation, which are encoded in the body by means of cellular memory. Among these are automatic behavior patterns which flow from that which we call premature cognitive commitments. These are promises made by an individual to the self or to others during early childhood, infancy, gestation, or even in past lives. Many of these long-forgotten promises are no longer - or never really were - valid as working tools on which to pattern one's general behavior.

Deeply buried early memories, including pre-birth recollection, are a leading cause for dis-ease. This particular need for personal healing is addressed by psychotherapy, rebirthing, various forms of healing the inner child, Healing Touch Therapy[1] and so forth.

Personal good health is an expression of balance between body, mind and spirit. As new challenges appear and manifest in your personal lives and along your individual paths toward full self-realization, a constant need for re-balancing is generated.

As you assist others in stimulating and encouraging their self-healing (balancing) processes, your own need for healing /balancing is both stimulated and served. As you assist others in addressing their problems and in setting their feet more firmly on the path of enlightenment, your own problems are both manifested and addressed. Your own feet are more swift and sure upon your chosen path. All healing is self-healing.

Sources of Dis-Ease

The causes of illness and imbalance are many, and often complex. **Any given illness or injury usually stems from a combination of several interrelated causes.**

The higher self programs specific challenges to be undergone during a given incarnation. These challenges often take the form of physically manifested illness or injury. To the extent that these here-and-now challenges relate to past life experience and past life choices, a causal factor is said to be *karmic.*

There are instances in which physical, mental or emotional

illness has been manifested in order to provide a challenge (and consequent opportunity for choice and growth) to others with whom the self is interactive in a given incarnation. In addition, many who have chosen various levels of service as teachers and Light-workers have manifested illness or injury in their lives in order to be able to say to someone else, "I know how it is. I've been there," or otherwise as a statement of personal imperfection. Imperfection lends credibility to the teacher or healer; people in need don't relate well to someone who is too perfect. These causal factors are said to be *dharmic.*

The healer of primitive earthplane tradition, the shaman, is called "the wounded healer." Shamanic initiation is often the province of those who have been physically impaired or sickly from birth, or it is precipitated by onset of sudden illness or debilitating condition.[2]

In many primitive cultures, priestly (shamanic) initiation was ritualized within a process symbolizing death and resurrection. Having first ventured into the spirit worlds both above and below the earth, the priest or shaman was thereafter viewed as a spirit being, uniquely able to conduct the affairs of the tribe on lower world, middle world, and upper world levels.

In modern times, many persons have been drawn to a practice of healing following an *actual* death and resurrection experience, which is sometimes mistakenly called a "near death experience."

In the potential healing practitioner, then, dis-ease or other physical need for healing is usually manifested as an integral part of one's choice to serve as a healer. You must fully understand a dysfunctional system by participating in it at some level, to assist its healing.

Self-Healing Mirrors Earth-Healing

Issues in your personal and corporate (group, society, national and international) lives are mirrors of the Earth-planet's issues. As individuals you are under constant stress - so is the Earth. Your physical, intellectual, emotional and spiritual bodies are sharing the experience of the planet's physical, intellectual, emotional and spiritual bodies. Your auras are strongly linked to the auric and etheric bodies of the earth.

Now is the time of culmination of personal and planetary history alike. Lessons ignored or neglected at their first presentation have a way of resurfacing again and again until they are finally learned. The law of karma prevails until a balance is achieved - or until it is superseded by the laws of wisdom and grace. A history of unwise choices and unhealthy practices is coming home to roost. This is true for individuals, for groups, ethnic and philosophical constituencies, societies, nations, the human species, for the Earthplanet as a whole. It's time to learn those tired old lessons and get on with the renewal!

All healing is earth-healing. As you resolve your own personal concerns and achieve successively higher levels of balanced wellness for yourselves, you also raise the overall level of *global* health. As you learn and grow, the Earthplanet learns and grows. You are agents of the manifestation of mass consciousness, in which personal and common good are clearly perceived to be one and the same. We are many, and we are One.

Among the personal and planetary issues that mirror each other in your current lives and times are pollution (the overloading of the immune systems of your physical bodies and the planetary physical body), conflict relationships (everything from inner and interpersonal conflicts to wars and rumors of wars), the thrust for accelerated spiritual enlightenment and awakening of co-creatorship empowerment (personal and collective relationship to the Universal, and the planet's relationship to other units of the Cosmos), and so forth.

You are shedding the limitations of old perceptions and outworn teachings as a snake sheds its skin. You are emerging into a new dimension of yourSelf as surely as the Earthplanet is emerging through the age of transition into a new dimensional reality. As you overcome limitation in yourselves and integrate more fully with the energy of each individual Higher Self, you shepherd the Earthplanet into a balanced flow toward a new realization of the Higher expression of planetary self.

By choosing to be incarnate at this particular time in earth's growth process, you also chose to be a part of the healing and maturing of the planet. You chose to participate. You chose to experience a wide variety of events and conditions - some of which are aptly termed illness, dis-ease, injury, "bad luck" and so forth - not only as a further step toward your own balanced wholeness of sum-total-Self but also toward balancing the energies and experiences of the human species and the planet as a whole.

For example, the planet's past history is in process of being balanced and healed through the widespread participation of individuals in sharing past-life energies through vast collections of those we term "spiritual parents." We shall speak again of this, at greater length.

Spirit Attachment:
Vicarious Dis-ease, Vicarious Self-healing

One widely-shared common cause for illness, injury - and even death - in this age is called *spirit attachment.* Termed "possession" by Dr. Edith Fiore in her book, *The Unquiet Dead,* and by Dr. William Baldwin in a similar system of understanding, spirit attachment occurs when someone dies and doesn't complete the full journey to the Light.

Spirit attachment is so common as to be near-universal. Almost everyone has attachments or has had attachments at some time during the incarnation.

Entities can be attached to places, objects, people or other living creatures. Those attached to places and objects have often been referred to as "earthbound" spirits. Entities who attach to incarnate human bodies often do so in a misguided attempt to be non-dead; to hang onto their perception of life by attempting to experience it vicariously through another person. We recommend that you read *The Unquiet Dead* and/or similar works to gain insight into this type of spirit attachment.

The imposition of duality, commonly called demonic possession, is a more intense form of spirit attachment.

The concept of spirit attachment release can also be viewed as a way of separating out negative aspects of perceived self, to facilitate resolution and healing.

An even more prevalent challenge of the current age of transition is called *Magnetic Field Deficiency.* There has always been a close correlation between the earth's magnetic field and personal, inter-personal, interspecies and planetary wellness.[3]

The earth's magnetic field is now at its weakest point in 3,000 years.

The geomagnetic forces which automatically supported wellness just aren't there for you, these days. You are beset by all manner of ills which your bodies (and the bodies of your nonhuman fellow planetary inhabitants) can't throw off as easily as in decades, centuries and ages past.

In the scientific community of your society, there is even growing speculation about whether *any* lifeform can survive on this planet, if the field is further weakened.

You can expect a number of consequences from Magnetic Field Deficiency. Among these are shortened lifespans for pets and domestic animals, reports of unexplained deaths of zoo animals and wildlife, a heightened incidence of extinction of various wildlife species, higher levels of physical discomfort (aches and pains, minor ailments) for human and nonhuman species alike, increasing difficulty in the management of chronic conditions or disabilities, and a general prevalence of immunological disorders - including AIDS - and other ills.

There will also be more beached whales and other instances of atypical behavior of aquatic mammals. The whales' internal navigational system is based partly on the sensing of the geomagnetic field, which is widely disturbed. There will also be instances of atypical self-endangering behavior by flocks of fowl as well as individual birds, and widespread anomalies in the migration patterns of land animals.

How can you combat Magnetic Field Deficiency Syndrome? Synchronicity is already at work! Information on magnets and magnetics is coming into your sphere of attention from many sources. There was an intriguing medical advance report on national network television a few weeks ago detailing how leukemia patients are being treated by having blood removed from their bodies **which is purified of cancer cells by being placed in a magnetic field** and then returned to their veins.

An article published in the New England Medical Journal was entitled "Can Cancer Cells Live in a Magnetic Field?" Small wonder that there is a growing interest in the use of magnetic products in support of personal healing and the maintenance of personal wellbeing!

Illness or injury can also stem directly from other aspects of the *shifting earth energies* which mark the current era of transition.

There is a deep interconnection between Universal energy, earth energy and personal energy: the planet's rising vibrational frequency has direct correlative effect on the bodies, minds and spirits of this sphere's inhabitants. These transitional energy shifts typically manifest in short-term personal adjustment phenomena such as headache, nausea, dizziness, ringing in the ears, irritability, and assorted aches and pains where there were none known to have been before, plus a feeling or urgency that leads you to want to resolve your problems **now.** This factor is sometimes referred to in oversimplified terms as ***stress.***

Stress from personal relationships and national or international affairs also falls into this category, as a central manifestation of the shifting vibrational planetary frequencies in the age of transition.

Another closely related causal factor is that of *negative energy wave flow*,[4] during which the destabilization of earth energies (for the ultimate purpose of restabilization at a higher frequency) is at periodic peak impact. During this particular energy realignment/destabilization phase, the planet is bombarded with negative impulses while its usual shielding is temporarily diminished. These negative impulses gravitate toward personal weaknesses (whether of body, mind, spirit or combinations of imbalance) and may or may not be intentionally harnessed and directed by sentient entities (whether incarnate or discarnate). This is another form of ***stress.***

The use of negative energy as tools for inappropriate personal expression and self-aggrandizement constitutes *psychic attack*[4], which can be a direct causal factor in manifestation of illness or injury. It almost invariably lowers an individual's overall balance of health so as to render him or her more vulnerable to the negative impact of other causal factors, related or unrelated. Psychic attack can be consciously or unconsciously directed, and lowers the resistance of both the recipient and the sender.

Happily, the incidence of psychic attack is being steadily reduced. More individuals and groups are aligning themselves firmly with the highest good within themselves, realigning\

balancing the free-willed separate self with Universal Oneness flow. Unhappily, the relatively small incidence of psychic attack which is still being practiced can be quite troublesome and often requires direct protective action to resolve it satisfactorily.

Another cause of illness/imbalance is the *assumption of someone else's problems in a subconscious attempt to resolve them vicariously.* Healers and other Lightworkers are particularly prone to this problem and must constantly clear themselves of negative energy buildup which may have been acquired during the course of their work or in interaction with friends and family.

Chapter 3

THE DYNAMICS OF SELF-HEALING

All healing is self-healing. Healing cannot be imposed on one person by another; the receiver must participate in the healing process or it will be ineffective.

Healers, how many times have you poured out healing energy on someone who was lukewarm about the process, only to have their recovery prove short-lived? How many times have you extended yourself in offering healing to someone who didn't ask for it or offer an exchange of energies for it, only to find they received little or no benefit from it? The recipient must make an *investment* in self-healing, as a statement of intent.

The intent for self-healing is a necessary foundation for change; in its absence any symptomatic relief will be short-term. If someone has chosen illness as a karmic challenge they won't give it up until they feel the lesson has been learned. If someone has inwardly agreed to provide growth opportunity lessons to others in their lives, they will not abandon that effort until and unless they are satisfied they have done their best.

Those who are intentionally participating in earth-healing through mirroring, sharing and healing planetary issues will likely continue doing so until they feel a purpose has been met and/or until they develop new ways of service that are effectively self-healing rather than unconsciously self-destructive.

If someone has truly made the choice to prepare for the death crossing transition, then no amount of external pressure for healing will avert eventual death.

Let us note that the death crossing transition is by no means always a negative choice. Often it is the natural manifestation of an incarnation's conclusion: a way of saying "I've finished this project; now it's time to move on to another." True healing is not just a simple avoidance of death or control of pain. It is the balancing of body, mind and spirit in such a way that the entity's progress along her or his chosen path is strengthened and facilitated. In many instances the death crossing transition is in and of itself a form of healing.

Traditional medicine has a tendency to focus on the preservation of the physical body - the current incarnation of an individual - as its sole goal. We regard this not only as an oversimplified view of healing, but as counterproductive to healing in some situations. Those who seek recognition of the individual's inherent "right to die" are expressing a viewpoint which affirms free will and the choice to make personal life/growthpath decisions without seeking a consensus. Free will cannot be frustrated indefinitely, in any case, especially when it is exercised on the basis of *informed choice* opportunity.

Traditional medicine has its place in the healing scheme, and is of great value in appropriate instances. Wholistic healing disciplines also offer various valid avenues for problem-solving and health enhancement. Neither traditional nor nontraditional healthcare can fully succeed without personal commitment: *All* healing is self-healing.

There is the clear need for spiritual guidance and counseling as a part of the healing process, particularly in the many instances where someone still needs to *understand* the situation in order to receive full benefit of the lesson being learned.

There are also a growing number of instances in which the problem's probable and possible root causes have been examined repeatedly, without bringing forth a resolution/release symptomatic manifestation. Over-zealousness in intellectualizing the situation may have led to "analysis paralysis" and the creation of a vicious circle of a no-win thought process.

Whatever one's history of conscious choices on the self-healing path, sometimes you come to a "stuck point." You lose momentum, the pace of self-healing progress diminishes, and you need a boost.

Short-cuts to Personal Healing and Wellness

Do you wish to experience an assisted, accelerated process of identifying and releasing stubborn longstanding blockages which often constitute the root of the problem? Are you willing to experience short-term psychological or emotional pain in order to achieve long-term gain for body, mind and spirit? If so, you may wish to consider therapies[5] which access cellular body memory with a view to identification, review and the release of premature cognitive commitments.

Are you ready to choose health instead of sickness; wholeness instead of injury or impairment? Are you ready to let go of your problems? Would you like to say, "Never mind why ... just let it go!"? This is a good time for that approach to healing! If your self-chosen lessons have been learned and assimilated and you are still stuck in a pattern of dis-ease or impairment largely through sheer force of habit, your intention for wellness, clearly stated, can be further supported by useful tools and techniques.

In our opinion, the strongest single self-care tool for self-healing support is magnetic healing. The strongest single, broadbase self-care technique for self-healing support is Reiki. Another excellent source of accelerated and intensive individual self-healing support is offered through our channels.[5] Other teachers of self-healing also offer valuable support services.

No matter what the cause or combination of causes responsible for creating illness, you *can* decide to "just let it go" and manifest good health. No matter why and how an imbalance has been created, you can achieve a balance of body, mind and spirit. Self-healing assistance from competent, caring people is often very helpful in accomplishing this in an accelerated flow.

Deepak Chopra's works, *Creating Health* and *Quantum Healing*, feature information on how and why it is within your grasp to manifest balanced wellness in your life, and in the life of the Earthplanet. There are also many other fine books available exploring, explaining and detailing the mind's ability to heal the body.

The first step toward wellness is the decision for self-healing; the second step is active implementation of that decision.

There is a quick and easy method of self-healing support readily available to you, even if you are not Reiki or Mahikari trained and have no convenient access to practitioners or teachers of those healing techniques or to others competent at core-level self-healing support.

Magnetic therapy is such a strong resource that we class it among the short-cuts to achieving and maintaining

wellness. There are a number of products on the market (and there will soon be more!) which support wellness through providing a magnetic field which interacts with body energy. The best of these are distributed in the United States through a company called Nikken.

How does magnetic healing work? The basics are simple: when you place a bar magnet across a blood vessel at a 90 degree angle, the positively charged ions in the blood gravitate toward one end of the magnet, and the negatively charged ions go for the other end. This is known as the Hall effect, which creates internal pressure on blood vessel walls, dilating the vessel and thus increasing circulation. Regardless of any other benefits which may also occur, increased circulation is foundational in allowing the body to heal itself.

Because bar magnets must be placed perpendicular to blood vessels for the Hall effect to manifest, and because blood vessels run in many different directions in the body, you can only reach about 15 percent of the blood vessels with a given bar magnet at any one time. So acupuncturists and others skilled in the practice of magnetic healing have traditionally moved bar magnets around on the body, placing them where they'll do the most good.

The strongest magnets are also quite expensive - costing about $30,000 for a pair of supermagnets generating a 25,000 gauss field for clinical use. Exposure to the field is usually rated at about one hour per day. Circular magnetic fields, such as those to be detailed below, are typically from 350 to 850 gauss in strength, with exposure time (as in sleeping overnight on a Nikken[3] mattress, for example) of six to eight hours or more.

Recent technological advances have made magnetic healing both more effective and affordable for self-care. In the 1970s, a German scientist whose career focus rested entirely on magnetic research and development came up with a way to produce a *circular* magnetic field.

By placing a North pole node at the center of the magnet and surrounding it consecutively with concentric rings of South, North and South pole nodes, a circular field is generated. When placed on the body, *at no matter what angle*, this field will cross from 92% to 100% of the blood vessels. This compares with a 15% efficiency rating for bar magnets, as previously stated, and is the basis for Nikken magnetic wellness-support products.

Nikken is a Japanese company which holds the license to distribute this patented product line, and has only recently started doing business in the United States. The firm has a 16-year track record in the Orient and elsewhere, and is rapidly expanding on a worldwide basis.

Another Nikken advantage is **affordability.** Their most expensive product is a king-sized mattress for $1,190, which compares favorably with the cost of premier quality nonmagnetic sleep systems. In Japan, one family in seven sleeps on Nikken sleep systems.

Their least expensive product is a small magnetic patch about the size of a silver dollar, which is applied to discomfort spots on the body such as those caused by tennis elbow, etc., or at the pressure points such as the sinus nodes, for relief of sinus headache and migraine. Other popular items include shoe insoles ($60 per pair), hand-held acupressure balls ($60), seat cushions ($120), and other items well within the financial reach of the average American family.

Nikken distributors market products on the basis of reducing stress and promoting a more restful sleep. They do not advertise medical benefits or claim "cures." While the product is certainly worthwhile on the basis of reducing discomfort and supporting restful sleep, many persons also report that they are experiencing higher levels of personal wellness support through its use.

How does a more restful sleep promote and support good health? According to Deepak Chopra in *Creating Health*, "Sleep is not only a state of consciousness, it is also an altered state of body chemistry; to go without sleeping and dreaming quickly creates severely abnormal brain functioning."

"Sleep deprivation quickly leads to loss of well-being," Chopra reports. "If experimental animals are deprived of sleep for even a few days, they die. In humans, sleep deprivation begins by causing fatigue, irritability and loss of concentration. It soon leads, however, to physical and mental disorientation, to delusions and hallucinations, and to a progressive decline in the ability to perform any coordinated movements at all."

According to Chopra, only about 57% of both men and women report they wake up feeling refreshed after a night's sleep (i.e., 43% do not regularly experience restful sleep), and about 25% of Americans need drugs to sleep, judging from the sale of sleeping aids.

Drug use to combat insomnia also has a characteristic drawback: drug tolerance. After a short period of use, sleep-inducing drugs become decreasingly effective.

As restful sleep and increased blood circulation are known to be foundational to the maintenance of physical and mental well-being, it makes good sense to consider the availability of wholly natural products that support wellness in these ways.

Magnetic healing - and the Nikken product line in particular - lends itself to widespread distribution in the mainstream marketplace of your culture, because it is based on demonstrable scientific principles. While those who are sensitive to energies are quick to tune in to magnetics instinctively, one need not be metaphysically awakened or espouse a particular belief system to experience benefits. You don't have to believe for it to work.

This is another reason for classing magnetic healing as a "shortcut" method - there need be no timelag for attitude adjustment to occur, before benefits are received.

Magnetic healing is proving increasingly effective in a broad range of application.[6] **It should also be noted that there are things it won't do.**

It won't override free will - when someone has chosen dis-ease, for whatever complex collection of conscious or unconscious reasons, magnetics won't automatically heal them anyway. They can still manifest dis-ease. However, *all* methods of reducing symptomatic discomfort - including the use of magnetics for that purpose - are likely to provide an atmosphere of greater comfort and clarity. Clarity often supports a choice for change.

Even for those who are preparing themselves for the death-crossing transition, magnetics and other healing tools and techniques are valuable in improving the quality of their remaining incarnational lifespan.

There is also the earth-healing aspect to consider: as the conscious exploration of magnetic therapy and attendant distribution and use of magnetic products becomes more widespread, this factor alone will reach a proportion great enough to be significant in supporting the stabilization and restoration of the planet's magnetic field.

There is a direct similarity between the ionic alignment that occurs in and through the human body in intentional hands-on or distance healing and that which occurs through exposure to strengthened/enhanced natural magnetic fields.[7] All healing is earth-healing.

Additional information on magnetic healing is surfacing in new books and theories, new products and ideas. Given the current and growing prevalence of Magnetic Deficiency Syndrome and its attendant increase in immunological disorders, you can expect this trend to continue for the foreseeable future.

The Role of Teachers and Healers

If you have chosen wellness and have the intention to implement that choice, there are many ways in which others can be of assistance in stimulating, encouraging and supporting your self-healing energies.

In primitive Earthplanet societies, the self-healing process for individuals and for the tribe integrated a combination of factors involving body, mind and spirit.

The pre-human, newly human and emergent human ***body*** went through a series of foundational genetic adaptations designed to support itself through a course of *actions* which became increasingly cerebrally-directed from one age to the next.

The human ***mind*** developed its intellectual capacity through a series of free will choice experiments (trial and error). Cleverness, creative problem-solving, the ability to work in cooperation with fellow humans and other creatures, the use of tools and general resourcefulness proved to be powerful assets in the evolutionary process known as "survival of the fittest."

Primitive ***spirit*** life (the conscious willful interaction with Universal Lifeforce, unseen/unfathomed presence and superhuman/metaphysical powers including those characterized as the forces of nature) was usually conducted through the symbolic and/or energy presence of god figures, including the power-personification of creatures and features of the world as they knew it.

Early humanity was attuned to recognition of power *outside* itself in the presence of animals, inanimate objects, sun, moon, stars, wind, and so forth. Feelings of self-empowerment came through personal, familial, clan or tribal association with external sources of strength, wisdom, or mystical force. The need to believe in something greater and wiser than oneself was foundationally instinctive in the human species and still permeates human understanding today.[8]

The tribal elder, medicine man or wisewoman, shaman, priestess/priest or teacher emerged as a resource on physical, mental and spiritual levels. These persons were perceived to be uniquely enabled through a special relationship with higher powers.

Humanity still turns to its leaders for self-healing support, practical advice, and spiritual guidance. Leadership roles have become progressively more complex, more sophisticated, and more specialized.

What are the hallmarks of a leader? From the beginning, those who serve in leadership roles have felt an inner call to do so: their personal destiny is inextricably linked with that of the community of which they are a part.

Their inner spiritual and intellectual need is to serve: to be of significant benefit to humanity and to Life itself. They are characteristically open to the consideration of new ideas and quick to seek bold new solutions to problems upon which they focus their attention.

Everyone has something to learn, and everyone has something to teach. Imperfect vessels also serve. However, those who exhibit the qualities of leadership are most likely to consistently be of assistance in supporting your growth and self-healing. It is your personal responsibility to be discerning in seeking out the teachers/leaders/co-creator associations and affinities which are right for you at any given point of your life/growthpath. Choose wisely!

In the present age of transition, the leadership cadre of Earthplanet's dominant species - humanity - also exhibits an additional feature: high energy. **By their fruits and by their energy you may know them.**

Of Benefit to Humankind

In a general review of Earthplanet history, you can see how qualities of leadership were manifested in body/mind/spirit balance through the ages of philosophy, religion, discovery, science, technology, and so forth. Think of the great discoverers and their discoveries in developing the means for a satisfying and abundant life, body, mind and spirit.

Think of those dedicated to the healing arts and the eradication or control of prevalent forms of dis-ease. Think of Hippocrates and Paracelsus, Fleming and VanLowenhoek; think of Pasteur and Salk, and others, from whose determination to seek and strive beyond the knowing of the common throng there have arisen a modern complexity of hospitals, research centers, specialized techniques and facilities in myriad forms. It is a system in which the focus is on preserving life, eliminating diseases through intervention in the physical (body) process, and it is/has been of enormous beneficial impact on the lifepath of the planet.

Then came the explorers and explorations of the powers of the mind and its interaction with body energy. Thanks to Freud and Mesmer and all the rest, you have the concept of "mental health" and psychoanalysis. The mind is acknowledged to be a powerful partner to the body, in creating and maintaining wellness.

Think of the Buddha and the Christ, and the founders of all faiths and philosophies! Think of your personal relationship to God, to the Universe and Universal. Think of the leaders who have come among you to show the way, to enLighten the path. Think of miracles and magic; of the knowing that there is more to humanity's Be-ing - and one's ability to heal oneself, to become whole - than just the mundane here and now.

Now we enter into an age of recognition of all three factors: body, mind and spirit, and the need for balance. It is an age of healing separations; an age of integration. It is a manifestation of Reunion, the fulfillment of promise and prophecy that we shall all become as One.

Self-healing and self-realization are requisites for Reunion. By freewill, there must be a clear *choice* to become as One. As an individual, you make that choice for yourself.

And as a dweller upon the Earthplanet, you participate in the process of *collective choice* for the planet. This collective choice process is called "mass consciousness".

All healing is self (chosen) healing. All healing is earth (chosen) healing, of which you are an integral part.

Chapter 4

PERSONAL WELLNESS
Self-Healing Tips for the Age of Transition

Whatever one's physical condition, it is always important to give attention to the balanced wellness of self: body, mind and spirit. The following recommendations are general in scope[9] and are appropriate for those whose physical bodies are in essentially good balance, as well as for those who are concerned for the care of acute or chronic health problems.

Deep Breathing Exercises: Vitalic Breathing

The average person's normal breathing process involves only about 30 percent to 80 percent of her or his lung capacity. In the largely inactive remaining portion of the lungs is a pocket of stale residual air which is seldom exchanged for fresh air. This pocket of habitually uncleansed and unpurified air contains not only a collection of environmental contaminants (e.g., traffic exhaust fumes, industrial fumes, tobacco, etc.) but also the "spent" body energies collected during the breathing and circulation process. This aggregation of toxins can - and does! - cause any number of physical problems, and it requires a strong percentage of personal energy to overcome or partially overcome its effects. It is detrimental to intellectual and spiritual well-being. Body, mind and spirit are all adversely affected.

Many people have accumulated toxins in the lungs well beyond their personal saturation points, and in consequence are now experiencing acute or chronic breathing problems. Virtually everyone has some level of lung contamination. Some are more naturally resistant to it than others. Regardless of the degree to which one's natural (unconscious) body defenses are developed and functioning, **these problems can be completely cleared up.**

An unaccustomed prevalence of volcanic dust in the atmosphere also has a tendency to irritate the lungs and worsen respiratory ills. As you know, volcanic activity is high during an era of transition such as the present age. You can expect this trend to continue, with an attendant need for stronger conscious focus on the clearing of the respiratory system.

Deep breathing exercises are an obvious first step toward cleansing and repurifying the lungs. These exercises should be done when the air is fresh and clean [never in polluted air – one wouldn't choose to do breathing exercises while sitting in an unventilated room, or in a car while stalled in heavy traffic!] and accompanied by visualization/imaging techniques designed to affirm the intention and understanding that a cleansing is taking place.

With every inhaled breath, visualize the crystal Light in oxygen molecules entering your body through the respiratory system. **The breath of God ... the breath of Life.**

If you don't have ready access to air you know to be clean and pure, purify the air around you by bringing Light through your body. Let it flow in at the crown, and out through your hands. If you are Reiki or Mahikari trained, you may wish to give Light to the neighborhood in which you live or work, using a photograph as a focus of intention.

With every exhale of breath, visualize the stale, spent energies flowing out of your body. **All the pain, the frustration, the anger, the old blockages ... let them go! Exhale them! Push them out!**

As you inhale, take in as much fresh air as you can possibly manage - and then just a little more! As you exhale, push out every last breath that you can manage - and then just a little bit more!

Aerobic exercises assist in stimulating the lungs in the exchange of stale air for fresh.

The breathing process by which the entire body is cleansed and renewed is also stimulated and benefitted by magnetic therapy, crystal healing exercises, aura cleansing and chakra balancing exercises, and other Light-focus meditations which generally promote wellness of body, mind and spirit.

Inhalation therapy, aromatherapy, diet and diet supplement therapies are also appropriate in many instances.

Inhaling the fumes of fresh ginger or fresh peppermint is helpful in clearing the breathing passages.

To do this, you would grate or pare a piece of fresh ginger into a cup or other small container and cover with boiling water. Let it steep a moment, covered, and then breathe the fumes. When you've gotten all the benefit you can from inhaling it, you can add a little honey to the steeped ginger water and drink the tea. Ginger fumes and ginger tea will also assist in maintaining mental clarity.

Peppermint fumes are prepared in the same way. Crush several sprigs of fresh peppermint into a cup or other container and cover with boiling water; let steep and breathe the fumes. Peppermint inhalation helps knock loose the sticky toxic scum that adheres to the interior walls of lungs and breathing passages. It will probably make you cough, and clear your sinuses! Peppermint tea is also an excellent digestive aid.

Relaxation and Self-affirmation

Meditation, relaxation, stress-reduction, self-affirmation, and self-empowerment techniques can be of significant benefit in promoting healing and wellness. (These include hypnosis, sleep-programming and subliminal audio and/or video tape recordings, providing they are correctly programmed and prepared by a responsible and effective narrator.)

Many excellent written resources[10] are also available as stimulants to self-affirmation, self-realization and effective meditation. The right resources for you are the ones which are most comfortable for you, and work best for you.

Don't be afraid to draw from several sources and craft your own combination of techniques. Experiment! Use creative combinations! Develop your own resources!

Cayenne and Other Hot Spicy Foods as Blood Purifiers

The use of certain spices as food preservatives in ages prior to the common practice of refrigeration - and in many parts of the world today where refrigeration is inaccessible or limited - has its direct correlation in body chemistry. "Hot" spices are useful in destroying bacteria, virus, and other impurities.

What is a "hot" spice? It is a substance that bypasses the sense of taste and goes directly to stimulation of the pain-sensing nerves of the body. It does not produce a scent or flavor, in the usual sense, but instead produces - in combination with body substances, when ingested or applied - a *chemical reaction.* When eaten it "tastes hot"; when applied to the skin or mucus membranes (usually quite by accident!) it is an irritant, often very painful.[11]

Unlike ginger, curry, cayenne and jalapeno derivatives, black and white peppers are only preservatives, not digestive aids, and should be avoided.

The routine use of hot spices as body purifiers is recommended for everyone, from those who seek a higher degree of wellness to those in the throes of life-threatening illness. This is a particularly important therapy for those who have AIDS or other immunological disorders. The spices won't kill the AIDS virus or otherwise cure immune system disorders, but they will assist in destroying impurities in the body that the immune system would have dealt with had it not been impaired.

We strongly suggest increasing one's taste and tolerance for hot spicy foods, the hotter the better!

Cayenne is an excellent example of a hot spice which aids in blood purification. Cayenne water may be prepared by putting two or three teaspoons of powder into a gallon pot of boiling water. Cool or refrigerate to drinking temperature, and take a small glass of cayenne water each day with a little lemon juice added. Honey may also be added as desired, without impairing the spice's efficiency as a purifying agent.

Hot spices are *blood* purifiers; they produce chemical substances which act directly in the blood. They also have a stimulating and cleansing effect on the digestive tract.

Another Simple Skin and Blood Purification Process

Environmental contaminants are universally distributed throughout the earth planet's atmosphere at this time, and have an impact on all the earth's lifeforms including incarnate human beings. Since many of these enter into the body through the breathing mechanisms of respiratory system and skin, fresh air deep-breathing exercises (as previously noted) and skin cleansing care are helpful in reducing their level of toxic impact on the physical system.

One significantly effective way of cleansing the skin and surface tissues - and to some degree the blood as well - is as follows: take some rolled oats and mix into a paste with lemon juice, using a small amount of water added if needed. The lemon juice need not be fresh, and may be bottled or frozen.

Scrub the skin thoroughly with oatmeal-lemon paste, over the whole body. Leave the paste on the body for five to ten minutes. Scrape the paste off and discard it; rinse with plain water. For detoxification, this should be done three times a week for two weeks, followed by twice a week for another two weeks and once a week for eight weeks. Once a month thereafter will help to maintain a healthy skin and reduce the level of blood contaminants.

The lemon juice helps draw the poisons out of the system and the oatmeal absorbs and removes it.

There are also oatmeal soaps commercially available which offer many of the same benefits.

Mud or mineral baths and sand scrubs are also effective in cleansing the pores of the skin and stimulating higher levels of healthy skin function, providing the mud, mineral waters or sand in question are not contaminated. Sea salt baths also prove helpful in many instances.

Vinegar baths and hot ginger baths (using grated fresh ginger) can be taken to clear the feeling of scummy residue in the wake of exposure to densely negative energies or the release of old dense blockages.

Cleansing of the Gastrointestinal Tract

The American Medical Association estimates that 40 percent to 60 percent of all disease is caused by impurities lodged in the colon. It has even been theorized that improperly working bowels may be a leading cause of most of the problems on the face of the earth. Mucus-forming foods, junk foods, white flour and bad digestion cause a buildup of a sticky substance which, along with existing accumulated waste matter, adheres to the walls of the intestines and colon.

As the walls of the colon become coated with these heavy substances, nutrition is restricted and other problems frequently arise.

When the digestive system is clean and functions smoothly, overall body health is often readily maintained. Through continuous neglect, however, the colon and other organs can become a source of poisoning for the whole body.

Environmental toxins are ingested daily, and many of the natural foods which traditionally assisted in maintaining inner body health have lapsed from common usage or have become ineffective through over-refinement.

For cleansing and maintenance of the colon, intestines, kidneys and gallbladder, we recommend you consider using products specifically designed for this purpose. There are several beneficial ones on the market. The best, in our opinion, is ReNeu, by First Fitness. Red Clover Combination is also an effective inner cleanser, although sometimes considered harsh, unmanageable, unpredictable or inconvenient for regular use.

The need for detoxification of the intestinal system is more pronounced in some persons than in others. Present-day exposure to environmental contaminants guarantees that everyone will have *some* level of need for internal cleansing.

Internal use of castor oil, mineral oil and similar oil-based laxatives assists in cleaning the digestive tract itself, but often does little to actually draw poisons out of the intestinal walls. Products which specifically address this problem, made of combinations of natural substances such as psyllium husks, are our recommended preference. However, laxative fruits, seeds and nuts (pumpkin seeds, sunflower seeds, dried fruits, trail mix, etc.) also often contain catalytical agents which assist in releasing toxins through the walls of the intestine, and we also consider them valuable for cleansing.

Beets and beet root powder also contain catalytic substances which promote deep-tissue detoxification.

High-fiber diets or diet supplements may or may not be high in toxin-drawing elements, depending on how they were processed. Use your instincts! Natural products are preferable.[12]

Release of Spirit Attachments

We recommend Dr. Edith Fiore's somewhat outdated, but highly informative book, *The Unquiet Dead*, and/or works by Dr. William Baldwin and others as background reading on the subject of spirit attachment.[4]

What is 'spirit attachment'? We use the term to designate units of negative, confused, stagnated, accumulated or otherwise "unreleased" entities or energies which have become lodged within the earthplane's third dimensional reality, and have become associated with or "attached to" persons, objects, or places.

There are three basic categories of spirit attachment: *simple entity attachment*, *possession*, and *energy attachment*.

Simple entity attachment typically manifests when someone dies, and, for whatever reasons, doesn't complete the death crossing transition into the Light (the spiritplane) but instead remains within the earth's vibrational field. These misguided folk often attach themselves to a living person in an attempt to live vicariously through someone else. In the process of doing so they usually manifest physical, mental and/or spiritual illness upon the host.

Until and unless alerted to the possibility that spirit attachment may be responsible for some of their problems, the host or hostess to whom the discarnate entity is attached usually misperceives the illness or other disturbing quality to be his or her own.

Possession is a term some authors use interchangeably with "spirit attachment", which we feel more aptly applies to attachments by entities other than those previously physically incarnate, i.e. demonic possession, fallen angel energies, extraterrestrials,[13] elementals, or other essentially non-human sentient entities.

Energy attachments don't involve a willfully-attaching entity, per se, but are instead the stagnant vibrational residue of past events. For example, let us envision that you have burnt the breakfast toast, and have thrown it away. You have taken the burnt toast outside to the garbage or perhaps to the birds in your garden - it isn't in your kitchen anymore - yet the *smell* of burnt toast lingers in the room.

In a similar way, energies can linger in the earth's vibrational field for long periods of time until they are cleansed and released. Another illustration would be of dishes that have been washed but not rinsed: a soap scum lingers on them, and will remain indefinitely until it is rinsed away.

Attachments usually cause physical illness or impairment, and can also be responsible (or contributing factors) for mental illness, character disorders and spiritual disturbance.

The single most common symptom of attachment is low energy level. The release of attachments is a significant healing tool.

How widespread is the problem? We estimate that 93 percent of the present incarnate human population of the earth planet is carrying spirit attachment. Non-human lifeforms (especially those closely associated with humans, such as domestic pets) can also have attachments.

How difficult is it to correct? How long does it take to free someone (or a place or thing) of attachments? It varies. Multiple attachments (at the same site, or hosted by the same individual) are quite common and some of them are usually released more easily than others. Sometimes the therapeutic release is a swift one; sometimes it takes several months and is rather like peeling an onion, taking off one layer after another.

Once attachments have been released, can something be done to prevent a recurrence of the problem? Yes, there are several helpful steps for sealing off the aura from encroachment. Information on these will be given in the section on crystal balancing exercises.

Why is spirit attachment an issue in these times, when it has been less so in the past? As the planet's rising vibrational frequency precipitates certain adjustments, dividing lines between dimensional realities which seemed so sharp for so long have become blurred.

The veil between earthplane and spiritplane is extremely thin.

The same thin veil between your dimension and ours which allows easier crossplane access to facilitate channeling, psychic development, telepathy and other metaphysical avenues of *positive* application on the path to enlightenment and Oneness also allows easier crossplane access for any *negative*[4] or *confused* energies and exchanges.

Free will is the law of the Universe. That being the case, why would anyone permit themselves, unwittingly, to become the host or hostess for attaching entities, possessing entities or attaching energies? By **group** free will, those who chose to incarnate in this age agreed to deal with certain pressing problems, for the benefit of the planet. Attachment is one of those pressing problems.

The purpose of taking on attachments is to assist them toward release; to see them through to the Light. While it is true that attachments often gravitate toward those who have tendencies toward alcoholism, drug abuse, smoking or other addictions, one should not feel that having attachments is necessarily an indication of character weakness or unworthiness. On the contrary, the strongest and most dedicated Lightworkers often have heavyweight attachments. Bugs come to the Light. And those who are the strongest often take on the strongest challenges.

In the instance of *possession* or *imposition* - sometimes called "heavyweight" attachment - awareness of the problem is more prevalent today **because many of the entities in question are coming forward to be healed.** They have begun to sense that it is truly the age of completion, the age of which the heralds spoke, and are waiting to hear the good news confirmed by an outside source.

Duality as a parameter of earthplane consensus reality is now in the process of being eliminated. A return to Universal Oneness is in progress; a great reunion process has begun. Those entities who entered into duality did so willingly, to serve a useful purpose by providing negative tension for positive energy to push against. Resistance is a necessary tool for growth.

Those who entered into duality became negative power figures, serving the Light in a unique way. They were given the promise that a way home would always be open to them.

The promise has been kept. As the gates of Homecoming are opened before them, ever more clearly, many need reassurance that it is, truly, the age of completion, in which they can honorably return to the Universal I-Am presence. Their task is finished; the end of duality on this planet is at hand. That is the new good news they come forward to hear.

Release of attachments takes many forms. While there is much one can do to release or remove attachments from one's person, family, belongings and surroundings, it is usually best to seek the assistance of an appropriate practitioner or counselor.

Many attaching entities are ready to be released; all they really need is an open invitation and a little encouraging reassurance. In those instances, the following affirmation and invitation are often sufficient to bring response:

Dear one(s), we welcome you in Love and Light.
You are healed and forgiven; redeemed and restored.
You are not now nor were you ever truly a part of darkness.
You are filled with your own Higher Consciousness,
your Christ Self (or Light self)[14]
You are filled with Christ Light (the Light of the Universe),
Filled with Christ Love (the Love of the Universe).
You will be taken to your perfect place in the Universe.
Go in peace...Go in peace...Go in peace.

In other instances, the attachments may need further counseling and reassurance. These are individually crafted to fit each given situation and need. Some need to be called by name, so they know the message is really meant for them.

Invitation to return and be One with the Light, sincerely expressed, is an essential element of every release we facilitate. No-one is cast out or rejected; no-one is so distanced from the Light and Love of the Universe that a return cannot be accomplished. *All* are welcome, in the Light.

Spontaneous release of attachments often occurs during the course of healing workshops and earthhealing release meditations - the release of attaching energies from locales, followed by a strengthening and rebalancing of the energy grid in that area.

In some instances, there is a problem-solving element which must precede release of attachment. Some attaching entities have information which must be shared or discussed before release is accomplished; in rare instances it is deemed preferable to allow attachment to continue for a time, or indefinitely.

In those cases, there is usually a new agreement formed between the host and the attachment which contributes to the greater benefit and comfort of both parties.

In these unique transitional times, release of attachment can be a highly complex process. Empowered self-participation is always a crucial factor - one cannot release an attachment from another without permission, unless there is a clear guardianship/custodial relationship involved, or unless the attaching entity directly seeks release - yet we strongly recommend something other than the do-it-yourself approach to attachment release. A skilled professional can offer much beneficial expertise.

Chapter 5

CRYSTAL BALANCING EXERCISES

Crystals have piesoelectric properties. Crystal energy interacts with personal energy (and geomagnetic energy, solarmagnetic energy, etc.) by means of magnetic vibration, and can be a significant healing and wellness support tool.

The alignment of ionic response, according to the properties of magnetic attraction and repulsion which occurs in crystal balancing, is similar in character, process and purpose to magnetic therapy and direct body-flow Lightwork healing (i.e., Reiki, Mahikari, laying on of hands). Crystal healing benefits individuals, groups, society, and the Earthplanet itself, as do other forms of healing.

Each method of ionic alignment stimulation and rebalancing, (whether through the use of crystals, magnets, personal or interpersonal body-channeled Lightwork, etc.) has its own nuances and fine points. Each healing/balancing method also interacts with every other method, and the use of *combinations* of methods is particularly effective.

For example: If Reiki is given to someone who is lying on a magnetic mattress or mattress pad, the intensity, penetration and speed at which Reiki Light is assimilated is greatly enhanced. Place the mattress within a grid of crystal energy, and additional benefits accrue. Use crystals and/or magnets to augment your personal energy in Core Energetics, and you will find your "powers" strongly enhanced. Crystals and magnets can be also used as readily in mental/spiritual healing context as in body-healing alone.

We do not agree with those who advise against mixing energy sources. There are instances in which one form or format of aligning energy has advantages over other techniques or tools, yet for the most part all natural energy sources are compatible, each to the other.

Many crystal healers and other metaphysical practitioners

have developed their own techniques for integrating crystal energy into the healing process. There are also numerous resources available in the open marketplace which give information - some of it more valid than others - on crystal usage. At present, we will focus primarily on crystal exercises that anyone can benefit from and on crystal insights not likely to be available elsewhere.

To Stimulate Physical Healing:

Choose two crystals to work with. One should be clear quartz. The other may also be clear quartz, or you may wish to use rose quartz, amethyst, chrysocolla, bloodstone, or smoky quartz. Both crystals should be not less than three inches long, for optimum results. (This is not an inflexible rule - sometimes smaller crystals can be very powerful. Use your own judgment.)

Take either crystal in your right hand, with the point toward your fingertips (if single-terminated). Hold this about three to four inches above the crown chakra, above your head.

Take the other crystal in your left hand, point toward the fingertips, and hold it about three or four inches above your right hand which is holding the first crystal.

Keep your left hand parallel to your right.

Allow yourself to focus on a specific need for physical healing. Identify the chakra which is nearest to the problem area, for example, the solar plexus (yellow) chakra if the problem is in the digestive tract.

Visualize that chakra color - yellow, in our example - as you continue to hold the crystals above your head. You need not "see" it clearly with your mental vision; you may think of an object you know is clear, strong, bright yellow. Establish the *intention* of "seeing yellow" and it will be effective.

Now mix a strong bright healing *green* color (green for healing) in with your visualized yellow. Don't combine the colors to make yellow-green; instead see swirls of green mixed with swirls of yellow, as in a lollipop or marble cake.

Using the crystals in your hands to define its flow (right hand closer to the body; left hand parallel to it a few inches outboard), bring the yellow-green swirl of visualized color slowly down over your face and body, across *all* the chakras in turn, until the hands fall naturally to either side as they pass the root chakra.

The yellow-green swirl envelops you completely, filling your aura, wrapping you in a warm healing glow-blanket from head to toe. Allow yourself to feel the energy tug as the crystals in your hands approach and interact with each chakra in turn.

Allow yourself a moment of complete relaxation as you finish this portion of the exercise. Take a deep breath.

Now allow yourself to focus on any *other* need for physical healing, and identify the nearest chakra to it. Holding the crystals above your head as before, pull up the color of that chakra in your mind's eye (i.e., clear or turquoise blue for the throat chakra). Swirl in green, as before, and repeat the exercise.

Repeat the exercise for each body area that needs physical healing. For the heart chakra area, which is already green, you may wish to visualize either swirls of "double green" - like" double chocolate" - or swirl in the white or golden Light of the Universe.

To Balance the Chakras:

Using the same general process as in the healing exercise above, visualize the bright vibrant red of the root chakra. Swirl in violet, for wisdom, and complete the exercise.

Follow through by visualizing the color of each of the remaining chakras in turn, swirled with violet, and complete the exercise using the foregoing techniques.

When you reach the crown chakra, which is already violet, you may visualize "double violet", or swirl in deep rich magentapink (for Love) or white or golden Universal Light.

At the End of a Healing and/or Balancing Exercise:

Position the crystals in your right and left hands above your crown chakra, as before.

Visualize the clear white balanced Light of your own aura, your personal energy field. (All the colors together make white.)

Now visualize, affirm, and allow yourself to ***FEEL*** the white or golden column of Light that connects you to the Universe. As you complete the exercise by drawing this blanket of Light over your body and aura, be aware that you are connected to Universal Light; let the Light and Love of the All-That-Is flow freely in you and around you.

As your hands fall naturally to the sides upon passing the root chakra, take your hands and arms and *push your aura* as far away from your body as you can reach; extend it to its maximum range. Now *stir in Universal Light,* in a circular motion. Feel the energy.

When you finish, *pull your aura back in* to its normal position nearer your physical body, being aware that it has been compacted, strengthened, **filled with Light.**

Any portion of these exercises may be done alone or in combination with any other portion. It is not necessary to go through the whole set of exercises to benefit from portions of it, but many people choose to go through one full sequence once a day, perhaps upon arising or retiring, as a therapeutic process.

Toning or chanting may be used as an accompaniment to these crystal exercises, toward enhanced vibrational open flow.

If you do the exercises in the morning on arising, focus on the knowledge that they are self-affirming, uplifting, strengthening, exciting! You will have all the strength you need for the challenges of the day; you will be filled with joyful enthusiasm for the tasks that come your way.

In doing the exercises at night upon retiring, focus on knowing they are self-affirming, soothing, relaxing, and will promote a restful sleep from which you will awaken refreshed and renewed.

These exercises may be done in group as well as individual settings, and we encourage you to share these techniques with others who may wish to become aware of them.

A Blue "Sealer" Coat for the Aura:

When attachments and significant levels of blockage have been cleared (and not before!), you may wish to consider putting a "sealer" on the aura to deter further entity or energy attachment. This process should follow a full set of healing and balancing exercises (as given above), and should preferably be accomplished with the assistance of someone qualified to participate .

> Visualize the white or golden Light of the Universe continuing to flow into your aura and being, at the very center of your being. Affirm that this is a continual flow; you are always and forever a channel of Light. The Force is with you.
>
> Now visualize application of the blue sealer coat. It is the color of an Aqua Aura crystal, and crackles with sparkling Light energy. It is highly kinetic; always moving swiftly, flowing ceaselessly.
>
> The sealer is specifically *blue* because it relates to communication, and embodies a sort of prerecorded message beamed at any approaching entities or energies that might draw near with intention to attach. The prerecorded message says (in simple terms):
>
> > *"You can't come into the aura.*
> > *You cannot attach here.*
> > *Go to the Light, in Love.*
> > *It is never too late to choose the Light.*
> > *You will be accepted into the Light.*
> > *You will not be sent to hell.*
> > *You will not be annihilated.*
> > *You will be comforted, counseled, guided*
> > *and loved.*
> > *Go to the Light.*
> > *By free will of this individual, strengthened by*

the will of the Universe, you cannot enter here.
Go to the Light.
It is the age of completion, of which the heralds sang.
Return to the Light. Go home ... it is time."

NOTE: This "sealer" will deter any casual entities or energies looking for someone to attach to, but will *not* prevent the assumption of any attachments you (or your higher self) may choose to admit, by free will.

The Use of "Sucking" Crystals:

Some crystals can be used to draw off poisons through the skin, and absorb them into the crystal.

Amethysts (especially the new Guadelajara amethysts, with their characteristically rough surface and complex interior energies), rose quartz, appetite, hematite, obsidian, most tektites, dark smoky quartz, chrysocolla, lapis, bloodstone, amber, and a number of others can often be used for this purpose. However, not every crystal in a given category has "sucking" power - use your own instincts to choose a sucking crystal, or seek guidance from someone whose instincts you trust. Guadelajara amethysts always suck; so do red and/or blue phantoms. Red and blue phantoms - including crystals with inclusions that aren't perfect phantoms - are ideally used in pairs, one red and one blue, opposite each other. (See below.) The use of a sucking crystal can be a substitute for the hot castor oil pack therapies recommended in the Cayce readings, especially if the focal point of injury, illness or distress is relatively narrow and localized. Hot castor oil packs are still effective - the crystals are less messy.

Depending on the site of the problem, we recommend taping a small sucking crystal to the body at that location and leaving it on overnight. The therapeutic value of this procedure can be enhanced by programming oneself (that is, by asking the higher self and guides to participate) to do intensive self-healing work while in dream state.

Use common sense! Don't tape it to the body where rolling on it would cause irritation or injury; don't use this method on small children or others who might swallow the crystal or otherwise misuse it to their detriment!

Sucking crystals should always be cleansed thoroughly after each use. This may be done by smudging, fire purification (holding them over a flame), washing in clear water with an affirmation, soaking in salt/sage water, or other cleansing techniques.

The Use of Red and Blue Inclusion Energies as Cleansers and/or Healing Energy Stimulants:

Choose a quartz crystal with red inclusions for one hand and one with blue inclusions for the other. It doesn't matter which one goes in which hand; suit yourself.

Lie down face up, at full length, in a comfortable position. Use pillows at the head, knees or elsewhere as desired. **Make yourself comfortable!**

Call in the Light, allowing it to enter through the crown chakra and/or the crown portion of the aura. Direct the spent, stagnant, stale or negative energies to flow out of the body through the chakras at the sole of each foot. Be willing to give the spent energies to the earth, knowing they will be purified and rendered harmless at the earth's molten core. Send them all the way to the core; visualize the molten core.

Allow the energy to flow throughout your body. Holding one crystal in each hand closes the electromagnetic circuit and facilitates an enhanced energy flow.

Feel the warmth. Allow yourself to accept the understanding that you *will* experience healing. Set aside any doubts you may have, at least for the moment - if you want them back again you can always recall them. For the moment set them aside.

Allow your self-healing energies to flow.

You may wish to use relaxing music, or a pleasing incense. You may meditate in whatever way feels comfortable to you. Just don't get so caught up in a meditation technique that you cease to feel the warm energy flow.

Breathe in Light with every breath the breath of God, the breath of Life. With every exhale, let go the blockages, fears, pain, frustrations, all the negatives and confusion ... breath it out. Breathe in Light ... breathe out the stale spent energies; all the undesirables. Let them go!

Other Crystal Usages That Can Be Combined With Red/Blue Inclusion Pairings or Used Independently:

Clear quartz or other crystals may be substituted for the red/blue inclusion pairs as given above. It is important to hold a crystal in each hand to close the electromagnetic circuit through the body.

1. Place a crystal or line of crystals across the soles of both feet, connecting the energy flow through the feet. This recirculation of positive energy will not interfere with the release of negative energy out the chakras of the feet.

   Crystals may also be placed on each chakra. Double-terminated crystals are especially good for placing on the chakras, and other stones of various types may be used.

   For use of colored stones in healing layouts (either placed on the chakras or in an arrangement representing the chakras), a general rule of thumb is that one can use stones the same color as the chakra in question. Further information on use of stones is to be found in the crystals and stones listing section of this document.

2. Place a generator, teacher or master crystal above the crown, and a large sucking crystal at the foot of the body, centered equidistant from each foot, *not quite* touching the feet. At the outside edge of the small toe of each foot, place a smaller sucking crystal and point it inward toward the larger sucking crystal centered just beyond the feet.

3. Do your healing meditation and crystal exercises within a crystal-defined energy grid or with the assistance of a crystal "layout." You may wish to ask some qualified person to help you with the selection and arrangement of crystals.

4. With a crystal in each hand, do some stretching exercises. (These may be done in standing position as well as lying down, but should be low-stress and relaxed rather than high-impact and accelerated in tempo.) Stre-e-e-tch your body ... allow the warm Light to flow in between the vertebrae and into the joints; allow the healing energies to penetrate deeply into muscles and other body tissues.

5. In a prone position with crystals in each hand and others placed about you and/or on the chakras, as you may wish, complete the relaxation and stimulated energy-flow portion of the exercise. Now take a *very* deep breath, breathing in Light, and hold it ... to a count of seven. On the count of seven, release the inheld breath of Light sharply and forcefully, directing it like a bolt of lightning directly to the part of your body that most needs the healing energy. Repeat this seven times. Now breathe in Light and hold to the count of seven again, and this time let the out-breath be gentle and controlled, pushing it gently toward the part of the body that needs healing. H..E..A..L..I..N..G! Let it flow!

These crystal exercise techniques may easily be combined with color visualization and/or toning. They will also be enhanced by doing them on a magnetic mattress or pad.

Chapter 6

CLEARING THE TOXINS FROM YOUR BODY AND YOUR LIFE

The toxins you are exposed to in modern society come in many subtle shapes and sizes. Some are quite obvious: vehicle and industrial exhaust fumes, chemical pollution, 60-cycle electrical vibration, reactive metals such as aluminum, food preservatives, substance abuse (whether so-called recreational drugs or socially acceptable prescription or non-prescription items), natural and man-made radiations, and so forth. There is abundant literature and counsel available on recognizing, managing and clearing these toxins from your body.

Specific remedies for specific toxic contaminations are available through herbologists, homeopaths, nutritionists, some clairvoyants, and a wealth of self-help literature including that which has been drawn from the Edgar Cayce readings.

The equally prevalent impact of toxic thoughts, speech, habits, relationships, associations and customs of society is not quite so obvious. For assistance in recognizing, managing and clearing these toxins in your life you turn to literature, support groups, personal growth exploration and choose counselors such as psychologists, intuitive counselors, rebirthers, and spiritual teachers.

There are also a number of human potential trainings that raise consciousness on the focus of toxic habits, speech and interpersonal relationships. These come in all varieties. For every school of thought or avenue of exploration, there is a constituency that needs it. Be selective in choosing the right resource for *you*.

Abundant insight on tools and techniques for generalized clearing of toxins is offered in this work and elsewhere. For example: we have mentioned ReNeu and other internal body aids, magnetic therapy, crystal healing, Hands of Light, Reiki, Mahikari, and other overall purification/self-healing techniques.

With the exception of the ReNeu and other agents that interact primarily with the body only, all these resources support the direct whole-self's clearing of toxins from body, mind and spirit.

Clearing toxins is a matter of changing vibrations or shifting polarities to elicit a whole-self response in body, mind and spirit. Vibrational changes and polarity realignment are facilitated by the intentional and/or spontaneous interactions stemming from the use of crystals, magnets, and/or an interaction of energies through the healer's human body.

Massage Therapy

Bodywork is very helpful in moving energies through the body. Self-healing energies are stimulated and the release of negatives/blockages is facilitated. While almost any massage therapist is better than none, it is particularly helpful to avail oneself of the services of a therapist who combines Lightwork - direct energy therapy - with massage. Some therapists also counsel, and many use music and/or aromatherapy in conjunction with massage.

In any instance where *touch* is used in healing/wellness support, it is of additional benefit to also use crystals in grid or other arrangement, to practice Lightwork techniques and/or to stimulate energy flow and blood circulation through the use of magnets. Nikken magnetic mattress pads are growing in popularity with massage therapists, and are available in custom-made sizes to fit massage tables.

Many massage therapists are also Reiki practitioners, as are a growing number of chiropractors, nurses, physicians and other healthcare professionals. In most European, Oriental and South American nations, Reiki and Mahikari are recognized as adjunct techniques which support other traditional and non-traditional healing methods.

Thai Massage is focused directly on stimulating flow through energy meridians and clearing blocked energy points in the body. Even without a counseling interchange to accompany the massage, clients often experience a resurgence of long-buried memory relating to blockages, or go through an emotional and/or physical cleansing-response as blocked energies are released.

Chiropractic Manipulation

As in massage therapy, it is particularly beneficial to seek the services of a qualified chiropractor who is also a Light-worker and brings energy through the hands. A significantly high number of chiropractors *are* consciously aware of this Lightbringing aspect of their work, and there are also those who bring energy without being consciously aware of it.

Blessing/Energizing Food and Drink

Energy is a blessing, and blessing is an energy.

"Blessing" is a bringing-Light; a sharing of energy; an affirmation of a personal and interpersonal connection to Universal Light, a manifestation of "The Force."

Energy/blessing flows through the human aura/body, usually entering at the crown, and radiates from the palms. Think how this understanding is reflected in artwork or recorded history. He raised his hands and blessed them ... the blessing of rain falling on a parched earth whose beings lift up their leaves and blades to receive it ... a child reaching up for Mother's arms, to be blessed by her Love ...

The blessing of food and drink was, in olden times, a process of *purification*, by focusing Light energy through the palms toward that which was to be consumed. Although a fuller understanding of the energy aspect of blessing has largely been lost over the years, blessing is still a purification. The *intention* of blessing brings purification. The poorest, meanest or most foul substance can be successfully purified and dedicated to the sustenance of your body, by being blessed.

In this time of high levels of contaminants in virtually all food and drink that is available to you, blessing that which you consume - bringing Light energy to it, through your hands - is a highly effective means of purifying substances to be ingested into your body. The psychological aspect of saying grace will also assist in attuning you to the earth and the fruits of the earth, aligning your positive energy with that of the Earth-Mother, the planet itself.

A Joyful Exuberance and Love of Life, As Self-Healing Force

This is perhaps the most effective healing agent of all. Allow yourselves *joy*, and health will come more easily.

Affirm the wonder of the gift of life by affirming your own aliveness; *be joyful!*

For too long, you have misperceived that spirituality comes through pain and self denial; through not doing what makes you joyful and through doing that which is not pleasurable to you.

We say to you now, to those who will listen and choose to hear, that fulfillment and ascension will not come through pain, but through joy. Spiritual realization will not come through self-denial, but through self-affirmation. Service to others does not come through self-denigration, but through self-empowerment!

Assisting the self-healing of others is in large part a process of encouraging their self-empowerment ... and you can't give what you don't have.

Have joy, that you may also give it! Acknowledge that you are a powerful Be-ing, that you may assist in stimulating the self-empowerment of others!

Good health is not promoted by a grudging dull following of rules and regimen, but by a full open-hearted zest for life - a *partaking* of the fruits of life, body, mind and spirit.

As Deepak Chopra puts it in *Creating Health*, health flows from granting your own desires; from wanting things that are good for you.

What is good health? It is a balanced partnership - body, mind and spirit. Ill health is an imbalance in which one aspect of the partnership - body, mind, spirit - dominates the others.

In ages past when Masters and Fully Realized Ones came upon the earth and walked among incarnates teaching, healing and comforting them, what messages did they bring to instruct and stimulate the populace toward balanced physical, mental and spiritual health?

The Buddha advocated the Middle Way - moderation in all things - yet many Buddhists express their spirituality and seek Oneness through transcendence (denial) of the body's needs and those of the mind as well. Spirit is all.

And what of the Christ and others, who said "... renounce the vain desires of the flesh!" Why were those teachings given? Because in those times, the people's body/mind/spirit partnership was clearly *out of balance.*

The body was dominant, often riding roughshod over mind and spirit. The teachings were given, saying, "... Look here, you've got to maintain a balance! Don't just go with what the body appetite is asking for; use your head! And be guided by spiritual principles!" Those teachings were sorely needed, and have been of great benefit to humanity - in spite of all the times and all the ways they have been misinterpreted and misapplied.

And what has happened since that time? We have come through a growth process as individuals, groups, nations, and a planet. We have come through a time when *mind* has been the dominant force, over body and spirit. Another imbalance. Science and technology ruled; the industrial revolution transformed the world. High-tech solutions were/are sought for every conceivable human need - including physical and spiritual health. Today's overdeveloped, overextended high-tech healthcare system is an excellent case in point. It relies heavily on chemical and/or technological intervention in bodily process to facilitate change.

Now, you are instinctively awakening to *spiritual* needs. Intellect isn't enough; there has to be something more. There must be some meaning to your lives, a purpose for living that goes beyond just moving from today through tomorrow on the same narrow path. You feel a need to relate to others; to your higher self; to the Universe. To know where you fit in. This is emergence of the *spirit* portion of your personal body / mind / spirit partnership.

And what of the body? You say the body is very much an integral part of your growth; you are healing and refining the body, yes? And are you allowing your body to give you *feedback?* Are you honoring the body's requests and considering the body's demonstrated needs? Or are the mind and spirit always telling the poor old body, "Do this! Do that! Be this! Be perfect!"

It is our opinion that many of you are out of balance again ... and this time it is the body that's getting the short end of the stick.

Allow the body - including the emotional body, which contains your sorrow, frustration and your capacity for joyfulness - to become a full working partner again, and you will experience great self-healing.

Feel the joy! Do things that make you happy! Nourish and nurture yourself! Do not continually set all your own needs aside in favor of the needs of others. If you do this, giving of yourself and never replenishing yourself by partaking of the gifts of the Universe, then one day you'll be all spent and have nothing left to give.

All healing is self-healing, and all healing is earth-healing. For a long time you have consciously or unconsciously shared the earth's pain, and we love you for your willingness to do this. But even as you have shared the earth's pain, know now that you must also share the earth's joy ... the healing cannot come by pain alone. There must be joy. We invite and encourage you to be a part of it.

Chapter 7

HEALTHCARE CRISIS IN AMERICA Circa 1980 - 2000

Your newspapers and television programs are filled with reports of failures of the present high-tech healthcare system, which is even now collapsing under its own weight. The same complex medicotechnological advances which have made organ transplants and microsurgeries a reality have carried with them a concurrently complex array of financial and ethical considerations.

Who shall receive fullscale all-out life support at its most intensive, most resourceful - and most expensive - availability? Everyone? Those who can afford to pay for it themselves, or for whom it will be paid from a collective fund, through an insurance carrier? Those whose need is most urgently critical? Those whose expectation for survival and significantly increased lifespan is highest? Those for whom the *quality* of life will be most improved? Do children take priority over seniors?

Do those who are contributing to their families and their society outrank the homeless derelict in the gutter? Or are all patients "equal" in the eye of the healthcare provider?

Is the patient's stated and/or demonstrated intention to continue the incarnation to be factored in at all?

The same pharmaceutical industry research and development process which has brought forth the creative chemical tools to conquer a long list of dis-eases is also conquering the bank accounts of a significant portion of the American public. Prescription drug costs have become burdensome (and in many instances prohibitive) for many segments of U.S. society, particularly the elderly.

Even non-prescription drugs such as pain blockers, cold/sinus remedies, antacids, laxatives, other digestive upset nostrums and sleeping aids can add up to a tidy sum in a monthly budget. Do you know what arthritics spend on anti-inflammatory agents and pain relief substances?

There are whole segments of your national society (to say nothing of those in other nations, worldwide!) that are being driven out of the high-tech and chemically-based healthcare market altogether. They just can't afford it. Yet many people have come to think of healthcare as a "right" that everyone should have regardless of personal financial circumstances. And they expect the government (or business/industry, or the wealthy, or charities) to pay for it.

There is clearly a healthcare crisis in America. And what's being done about it?

Apart from all the legislative, bureaucratic and official societal dithering about who's going to pay for what, what's being *done* about the healthcare crisis? A lot!

For one thing, there is a stronger focus on *prevention.* For another, greater numbers are seeking *alternative* health-support practitioners, techniques, remedies and tools. There is also growing recognition of roles of mind and spirit in creating bodily health, and *a growing awareness of the primacy of personal responsibility* - choice - in denying, seeking or creating a healthy balance.

There is a greater willingness to accept personal responsibility for the conscious or unconscious creation of one's own reality, and a new respect for the effect your desires, thoughts, speech and seemingly casual habits have on your health and the health of those around you. You are clearing toxins from your life - not only the obvious and tangible contaminants such as polluted air and water, toxic chemicals and food additives, but also the whole range of toxic relationships, speech, habits, and thoughts.

There is a widespread general shift from power-over based wellness/health support resources to those based on personal responsibility and choice, i.e., on power *within.*

YOU are very much a part of this major shift of consciousness. All healing is self-healing: *You* choose wellness; you choose the series of understandings, techniques, tools and teachers who support you in achieving and maintaining vibrant good health. All healing is earth- healing. As you support your own clearing of blockages and sloughing off of dis-eases and disabilities on the path to vibrant good health, you contribute significantly to the planet's shift from impairment to fulfillment.

There is no more important matter on the global plane-

tary agenda at this moment than your self-healing. *Your* self-healing is the only one you have full control over. Yes, there also are others around you whose self-healing you can stimulate, encourage, influence and support. Yes, they need your help - and we don't suggest that you cannot help them until and unless your own Be-ing is fully perfected. Ridiculous! One should not wait to be perfect in order to serve. Service is a part of the healing and perfecting process, on the path toward manifestation of essential Oneness.

Yes, there is a need for cooperative corporate governmental and societal action in many regards. Yes, your deep and generous caring for human constituencies, other lifeforms and for the Earth planet itself makes a difference.

And yes, your *personal* healing is a step in the right direction toward supporting those concerns. You are a living flame; an agent in creating and defining mass consciousness. **All healing is self-healing; all healing is earth-healing. The energies ARE that interconnected.**

You are integral parts of the maturation of the planet, agents of growth not only for the individual self-Be-ing but for the Earthplanet Be-ing as well. You are the agents of change whose action-supported choices are moving global society and the planet itself from the age of *power-over*, expressed in psychological aspects as well as in the application of scientific/technological principles and creativity, to a balanced system wherein body-mind-spirit elements all contribute toward solving the problems inherent in present day reality and co-creating the new reality.

The shift is from power-over to power-within. It is happening now and you are very much a part of it.

YOU are responsible for addressing the healthcare crisis in America, and in the world. National and global health begin with your own personal wellness.

You instinctively know this to be true. You are feeling a heightened inner impetus for greater responsibility in self-healing, making one's own decisions about health care and life choices.

Even in your speech and thought patterns you are shifting from power-over terminology to power-within. Instead of speaking of "winning the fight" against various dis-eases, you manifest or "create" wellness. The creative form is much more powerful than the conflictive. Affirmation of Life is far more powerful than denial of death.

You are less willing to follow doctor's orders blindly, "because she or he is the doctor," without an established rapport of proven trust and/or vibrational synchronicity between you.

You are instinctively questioning and rejecting a power-over approach to health care in which you give the decision-making process to the so-called experts and their reliance on the medical establishment's chemical and technological approach to wellness.

Where there is little or no practical alternative there is often a resentment; you feel uncomfortable at being asked to give away your power. Hospital care, for example, is so structured toward convenience of the staff rather than the patient that you feel restricted, dominated, even imprisoned or abused at being hospitalized.

Healthcare/wellness choices that affirm *power-within* attract your interest; an eagerness to learn more is welling up in you. Your own heart's knowledge and past life memories of self-healing/self- realization empowerment are flowing ever more freely, and you follow internal personal guidance in seeking those resources which support experience, exploration and expansion on these themes.

You instinctively feel drawn toward the growing mass of what are called "self-help" books and tapes. You attend fairs and expositions, placing yourself in a position to learn more about what's available. You gravitate toward seminars, workshops and classes, and to persons whose services can assist in supporting your growth toward wholeness. You join or form support groups such as healing, meditation, study or prayer circles.

You seek out combinations of teachers, tools and techniques that answer your needs.

The spiritual/metaphysical market is wide open. Be a smart shopper! Follow your inner guidance in choosing the resources that are right for you at any given point along the lifepath.

Chapter 8

SELF-VERIFICATION: BODY RESONANCE

The body *knows*. Everything you have ever done or felt or seen; everything you have ever perceived or thought; everything you have ever been or wanted to be or thought yourself to be is *embodied* in the cellular memory of your body. Even the past history of your unique essence in its journey from one lifetime to another is known to your body. The body knows the truth about the present, the past, and even about what the future is likely to hold.

As you tune in to body resonance you allow the knowing of the body to become more productively integrated with mind and spirit, toward a balanced wellness of the whole.

Listening to your body resonance is a matter of knowing what "rings true" for you.

Applied kinesiology is another method of using direct body response to provide veridical information. This is also sometimes called "muscle testing."

Reading Your Body

The body is an abundant source of information about itself.

Iridologists look to the eyes for placement and concentration of toxins throughout the whole body. Foot reflexologists will know what part of the body is out of balance according to which part of the foot is tight or tender. Physicians look at the hands and fingernails for clues to aid them in the diagnosis of disease.

Some who are skilled in the Ayurvedic and similar traditions of healing can do a full overview health scan simply by taking someone's pulse. And even the most unsophisticated observer will assume dark circles under someone's eyes to be an indication of insufficient sleep!

Body language offers additional clues as to the state of

someone's physical, emotional, mental and spiritual bodies.

As you become more aware of your own body responses and more observant of the body conditions and attitudes of others, you become more attuned to the flow of your own life and the lives of others. It is another of the steps toward mass consciousness, toward eventual Oneness.

Clarity and understanding bring cooperation, integration, Reunion. Lack of clarity and understanding promotes continued separation, conflict, and frustration.

Learning to read your body is a step toward learning to read the body of the earthplanet.

Individual body resonance is the source of personal knowing of truth; personal authority. Interconnective body resonance is the vehicle for manifesting mass consciousness, planetary healing. There is a bodily thrill of knowing, shared within a large or small group, that comes with right action - or even decision of *intent* to act.

This "thrill of knowing" is the physical manifestation of an energy-alignment in process of occurring. Once a wave of intention has been generated, it flows instantaneously to other persons and groups attuned to its principles. This is the process by which mass consciousness is manifested.

Learn to read your body. Tune in to your body resonance. Integrate the information of the body with that of mind and spirit for a swifter and fuller self-healing experience and for the healing of the planet.

In the process of doing this you will learn to communicate more productively with yourself, with others, and with the Universe.

Books and Tapes

As you consider the array of books or audio-visual products in your local bookstore, scan the available subject matter and let yourself be drawn to the areas of further exploration which seem most appealing to you. Stand quietly for a moment and center yourself in a place of self-communication. Tune in to *you.*

Now stretch out your hand with the intention that it is an instrument of sensing; a tool your inner self will use in guiding your eyes and thoughts to the right resources.

Reach out and pick up the book or tape toward which your hand naturally points. Examine it. Turn the book pages; read a few paragraphs. Audit or view samples of the tape if they are available. Consider the *feeling* you get from the product. Does it excite your interest? Does it feel like the right choice for you? If not or if you aren't sure, use the same process in considering the books or tape to either side nearby.

In choosing audiotapes or audiovisual aids, give careful consideration to the credentials, reputation and *energy* of the person or group who has prepared them. Discernment is particularly important when selecting subliminal or sleep-programming tapes.

When you have chosen and purchased a book or tape, remember that you are sometimes led to resources which aren't quite right for you yet, and will be exactly what you need in a few days or a few weeks. When you're ready, there they will be on your shelves waiting for you!

As you expand your self-exploration and build your library, you will identify topics in which your interest is more tightly focused, and authors whose insight and expression tends to be especially valuable to you on a continuing basis or at a given growth stage. As your growthpath continues, some authors /topics will continue to hold your interest, and others will seem to be "outgrown."

Remember your outgrown resources - including teachers - with appreciation for the roles they have played in your growth process, and use the insight you have gained about them, during your self-exploration, to guide you in making recommendations to others on their personal growthpaths. It often happens that the book or tape, teacher or technique which has become obsolete for your own needs is still highly valuable for someone you know.

Part of your emergence as a leader, teacher and healer has to do with sharing your experience and insight with others. In suggesting tools and techniques, books and tapes, teachers and healers to your friends you have the extended opportunity to further your own healing and growth by supporting the healing and growth of others.

Sometimes it's a big step for you to go out on the limb and suggest a "new age" book to a friend, or tell someone about a non-traditional healing technique you believe would benefit them. Being specific and direct in your recommendations has further advantages of exercising your self-expression, developing stronger interpersonal communication skills, fine-tuning your discernment toward broader leadership skills, and strengthening your confidence.

Always present your recommendations as suggestions for considerations, but never in a way that fails to acknowledge free will or affirms the principles of "power-over" (do-it-because-I-say-you-should). The power-over approach is spiritually incorrect, in our view. It also tends to be highly unproductive, setting up or crystallizing resistance in the very hearer whom you wished to influence.

A reading list and other recommendations for your consideration will be given at the end of this work. We encourage you to review it carefully, using your own best judgment and best instincts to identify which items will be of most benefit to you.

Gatherings

A great and well-loved Master once said, "Wherever two or more are gathered in My name, there I am also." And he said "Lo, I am with you always ... even unto the ends of the earth."

In speaking these words, the Christ was speaking in his role as Lightbringer, the Light of the world, the embodiment of positive LifeForce energy. He was an incarnate physical manifestation of "The Force."

The Light of the Universe is as near as your fingertips; you have only to reach out and let yourself receive ... let yourself *feel* the Light.

When you gather with others in a circle of growth or sharing, you share *energy* among yourselves, heart to heart and mind to mind. In the sharing process, each one has something to give and each one receives something in return.

In going to a gathering, sometimes you will be tuned to the opportunity to *give*. As a teacher or a healer, you will share your words and energy-presence with others ... and you will also receive from them, in the process of doing so.

As a student you go to *receive*. You will learn something from the speaker and from your fellow participants; you will benefit from their energy-presence. And you will also give to them, in the process of doing so.

The more open you are to both the giving and receiving aspects of a gathering, the more you facilitate a high level energy-sharing. The energy is interactive.

It is also exponential, rather than linear.

The energy you share with others in a gathering, large or small, adds up to more than just one plus one plus one ... it adds up in *multiples* according to the number and strength of the participants.

Sharing energy, one with another, also automatically evokes (calls forth) the Light within and invokes (calls forth) the Light of the Universe. In gathering and sharing, you will have instinctively opened yourself to the joy of Angels and Archangels, to the presence of Ascended Masters and LightBeings, to the flow of Universal LifeForce.

The Universe eagerly awaits your choice for self-healing and self-fulfillment. Your guides and teachers eagerly await the opportunity to share energy with you and others. As you gather, you call in the Force.

Wherever two or more are gathered in the name of the Light, there the Light will be.

It is always a good thing to be discriminating in your choice of gatherings, just as you are discerning in your choice of friends, guides, teachers, techniques, tools, and other spiritual growth resources. And you will "outgrow" some gatherings and circles of acquaintance, as you flow more swiftly and surely on your personal Lifepath.

As you learn, you will embrace your own swiftness without demanding that others keep pace. You will remember to bless them for what they are instead of blaming them for what they are not.

Chapter 9

PATTERNS OF HEALING

Everyone is a channel. Everyone can transcend the barrier between third and fourth dimensional vibrational frequencies, which are growing ever slighter, ever more permeable in the present age of transition. Channeling isn't just a sharing of spoken or written communication between earth and spirit-plane; it is a flow of energy.

Everyone is a channel through whom the LifeForce of the Cosmos flows. The Force is within you and all around you; there is only Brahman. All else is maya.

At the innnermost core of your Be-ing, you are attuned to Universal energy. You are the living crystals joining Father Sky to Mother Earth; you are the living magnets of planetary polarity realignment.

You radiate aspects of LifeForce energy with every step you take, with every thought you think, with every emotion you feel, with every soaring of the spirit, with every breath you inhale and exhale. For the sake of yourself and others, it is important to learn and practice one or more interactive *formats* in which the energy you radiate can be more clear, and can be shaped and projected in an orderly and efficient manner.

In this way you become a part of an interactive *gathering* which occurs in the etheric body of the earthplanet. Your shared energy transcends linear flow and becomes exponential.

Among the best known and most widely practiced formats of energy shaping and projecting in your society are prayer, meditation, ritual practice, corporate worship/fellowship and support group interaction. Couples, families and friendships are examples of support groups in which energy is shared and shaped.

The energy isn't always shaped and expressed in clearly positive ways. Sometimes the support you receive from others comes in the form of lesson-opportunity, or even adversarial interactions which test and ultimately strengthen you. In any event, **relationship interactions are exchanges of energy.**

Isn't it true that negative or confused relationships tend to drag you down, and positive relationships contribute to your wellness? These energy interactions usually occur naturally, without your being overly conscious of them.

Now you are becoming more *conscious* of every aspect of your lives and health. It is a good time to become consciously active in clearing, shaping and projecting energy.

It is a good time for focus on the self-healing of body, mind, spirit and earth. Healing techniques include those focused on the physical (bodywork, herbology, nutrition, etc.), mental (counseling, interactive sharing of thoughts and ideas), and spiritual (Lightwork, energetics).

Among Lightwork techniques for clearing, shaping and projecting energy of proven value are Reiki, Mahikari, and other methods in which Light is intentionally drawn into the body and projected from the hands.

Reiki and Mahikari are separate disciplines, taught and practiced separately.

Both Reiki and Mahikari are broadly recognized as adjuncts to traditional healing, worldwide, and practiced in Reiki or Mahikari healing centers in many countries.

Anyone can benefit from receiving Reiki and/or Mahikari and/or other Energetics techniques. Anyone can learn and practice Reiki and/or Mahikari and/or other Energetics techniques.

Mahikari

Mahikari, which means "True Light," is shared within the context of a carefully detailed process which includes ritual chanting. There is a powerful effect from tone and word-shape combinations which assists in allowing Light from the palms of the Mahikari giver to penetrate the etheric and astral bodies of the receiver more readily.

Healing occurs first in the etheric bodies, and then flows to the physical.

Mahikari (True Light) addresses the need for the clearing of entity attachments at direct energy level. Spirit attachments are presumed to be near-Universal in prevalence, and said to be responsible for about 85 percent of all physical dis-ease.

The attaching entities are healed and restored to Light or otherwise separated from the body by repeated applications of Light. Mahikari can correctly be described as (in part) an exorcistic model of a purification technique. The healing of body mind and spirit - including the healing of non-human species, food, water, other natural resources and the earth itself) flow from purification, i.e., from healing or removal of negative entity or energy attachments.

By means of ritual and the wearing of an empowered symbolic object, the Mahikari practitioner is protected from negative consequences through her or his intercessory interaction with negative energy fields and flows.

For more information, you may look to the Mahikari organization. If there is a Mahikari center in your city, it will be listed in the telephone directory. There are centers throughout the world, including many major U.S. cities such as San Francisco, Los Angeles, New York, Atlanta, Cincinnati and others.[14]

Mahikari teachings and practice are powerful healing techniques. Look to your own heart - your body resonance - to know whether this is a right avenue for your own self-healing exploration at this time.

Reiki

Reiki is one of the most immediate and satisfying tools available for personal transformation. Even if one does nothing more with Reiki except be initiated and do self-treatment, our world is healed by that factor of one.

Over 2,500 years old, Reiki is an ancient Zen Buddhist healing modality with roots in Tibet. "Reiki" (pronounced ray-key) is a Japanese term derived from *rei:* universal and *ki:* vital lifeforce. Thus, Reiki is a system of activating and utilizing the Universal Life Energy, the Force as channeled through an initiated and trained practitioner.

The awakening of latent natural LightForce access is called into play through an initiatory teaching of its tenets and symbols, coupled with the sharing of specific Reiki energy. The energy sharing initiation is called an *attunement*.

Attunements are transmitted by the meditation and touch

of a Reiki Master. They activate and align LifeForce energy safely and uniquely within the student's individual process. Use of Reiki is then taught through dialogue and experience.

Anyone can learn and benefit from Reiki. Beginners and advanced students alike will benefit from becoming Reiki trained, and children are often quite adept at it. Reiki practitioners learn how to apply, feel and work with this energy within the self and others. They experience significant life changes as they focus and enhance the personal transformative process.

Reiki practice also offers the intriguing opportunity to send Light across time as well as space. This specific Light-healing format is highly compatible with the practice of distance-healing and time-specific healing.

For more information on Reiki you may seek out the Reiki Masters in your own community, or contact: James Ben Stockton at (615) 791-8721.

Chakra Balancing, Auric Cleansing

There are many techniques for clearing and aligning body energies less specific than Reiki and Mahikari. Some of them are named and taught; many are self-developed and practiced within a wide range of traditions.

For example: Native American smudging is a purification rite which embodies the intention of its recipients and practitioners to be cleansed. It is therefore highly effective in clearing the aura and the area of free-floating negative energies.

Psychic Surgery

Psychic surgery differs from other Lightwork/Energetics techniques in that it generally goes beyond clearing blocked energies in the etheric body and auric fields (although this may also be a part of the process) and includes a reaching *into* the physical body.

Anyone can practice psychic surgery. You can do it on yourself as well as on others, and it is easily taught.

Psychic surgeons of the Philippine and certain other traditions are adept at aligning physical energies in such a way as to open the physical body, without pain. A high degree of trust is required between the surgeon and the client, whose understanding is prepared before the surgical process begins.

Psychic surgeons prepare themselves with appropriate meditations and other empowering techniques, before reaching into the body with their physical hands to remove impurities which are then discarded. During the process of preparing the client, negative energies have been stimulated toward coalescence into a quasi-physical form which can be grasped and moved. The body is then radiated with LightEnergy and allowed to heal itself.

Hands of Light

A less intrusive and equally effective form of psychic surgery is practiced by healers (teachers and supporters of self-healing) who do not physically open the subject's body.

One excellent resource for information on the non-invasive approach is Barbara Brennan's book *"Hands of Light."*

HOL (Hands-of-Light) healing is an aspect of W*holi*stic healing.

Using any one or any combination of methods which lend themselves to this practice, the healer first extends her or his etheric fingers beyond the physical hands, then gently and carefully moves the energy field of etheric fingers and etheric hands into the client's physical body-energy configuration.

When you perform HOL psychic surgery on someone, you will be surprised at how *tangible* the interior body energy-sensations are to your fingers, and how freely they stimulate images and sensations in your other senses of sight, sound, smell, taste. Anyone can learn to do this, and it is an excellent method of awakening your psychic sensing mechanisms more fully.[15]

When someone performs HOL psychic surgery on you, you will *feel* their fingers or hands inside your body. There will be no pain, no discomfort, only a sensation of energy moving inside you. Sometimes this sensation is perceived as heat, a prickly feeling, pressure, and so forth.

Blocked energies (sources of dis-ease; negative energy manifestations, accumulated at specific focal points in the body) are withdrawn from the physical and etheric bodies of the client and carefully disposed of by clearing them into the earth or sky, re-aligned and transmuted into Light.

Uncomfortable feelings such as nausea or weakness which sometimes accompany HOL procedures are a body response, *not* to the hands of the healer but to the negative energy release those hands have stimulated.

When a big chunk of blocked energy is dislodged by HOL it can have a powerful impact on the physical body. And even after the negative energies have been removed from the client's auric space to the highest possible degree, the body is typically still full of released toxins and undergoes some degree of cleansing syndrome.

Follow-Up Selfcare

Cleansing syndromes are common after powerful metaphysical healing experiences, whether planned and assisted or spontaneous happenings. They can sometimes be uncomfortable, yet if allowed to run their course without undue resistance they seldom last more than a day or two.

A cleansing response is definitely good news: a clear indication that changes are occurring. Healing is in progress!

For those whose auras are of average or below-average density, the more intensive the assisted self-healing experience, the more intensive the cleansing syndrome is likely to be.

Healing techniques such as the release of attachments, core energy work (Lightwork), and bodywork typically trigger physical adjustments which leave toxins in the bloodstream that need to be flushed out through the body's normal filtration systems. Counseling and/or accelerated internal self-examination and any consequent realignments can also trigger physical releaseresponse.

The body's cleansing (spent/negative energy release) mechanisms are:

- Direct energy release, through Lightwork process
- Excretion of waste through digestive and urinary tracts
- Sweating, shivering
- Coughing, sneezing
- Laughing, crying
- Deep breathing; aerobic exercise, including walking.

After an assisted self-healing experience, you'll get best results by encouraging the completion of your body's physical cleansing/releasing response.

Drink lots of clean water! This is a basic cleansing procedure that everyone should observe. You may also wish to drink quantities of fruit juices and teas.

Eat two medium apples a day, plus one medium sized raw potato. These are naturally detoxifying foods.

Cleansing of the outer body is beneficial. We recommend vinegar baths taken daily for at least three days after a major healing session, to remove the scum-like residue that can form on the skin. Oatmeal and lemon scrub is another excellent cleanser for deep-skin and the bloodstream.

Internal cleansing is important. For immediate detoxification, eat a medium-sized raw potato once a day, and two apples a day for at least three to seven days. Continue to eat one apple a day to prevent toxic buildup. Cayenne water is an excellent blood cleanser, and we recommend a product called ReNeu for general use in maintaining cleanliness of bowels and other internal organs.

Sweat! It's good for you. If you are a health club member, go and sit in the steam room or sauna. If you have no alcohol allergy or tendency toward dependency, you may wish to take hot lemonade with whiskey and honey in it; wrap up in a warm blanket and perspire profusely. Don't forget to replace the body's lost electrolytes afterward, with Gatorade or some other suitable substance! There is a product called Km which is generally beneficial and particularly helpful in establishing and maintaining electrolytic balance.

Cry if you want to! Tears from emotion have a different chemical composition than tears from eye irritation (such as onions); there is a cleansing element in them. If you feel the urge to cry, let go ... let it happen! **Don't hold back.** And don't feel you need to justify why you're crying; it doesn't matter *why*. Just let it run its course, and recognize that it's part of the healing follow-up process.

If you are driving down the highway and a song on the radio or some other happenstance makes you want to cry, pull over to the side of the road and *cry*. Don't repress it!

Get some extra sleep! Let the body do some of its release-adjustment while you're resting; you may even wish to program your dreams or ask your guides to assist you in accomplishing as much readjustment as possible during the dream state. This can be a powerful healing tool.

If you feel restless, **walk.** (If you're a runner, it's ok to run - but don't overextend yourself during a cleansing cycle, and don't take up running if you're not accustomed to it!)

Breathe deeply! If you can get out into a natural environment and enjoy the beauties of nature, so much the better. It will lift the spirits as well as the senses, and help restore healthy balance.

Talk about it with a *trusted* friend or counselor. Conversational give-and-take lets you express yourself and helps define your thoughts. You need to assimilate what you've learned; what the healing experience feels like and what it means to you. "Monday morning quarterbacking" can be an avenue for discovering new insights.

Don't repress anything! You can't rid yourself of pain, tensions or frustrations by denying them. Don't hold them back; process them and allow them to flow *through and out* of you, instead. Breathe in the Light and breathe out the spent energies, or let them flow into the earth through the chakras at the soles of the feet.

Don't be surprised if something new surfaces! After a healing session, you often become aware of something *else* that needs attention. When one pressing problem is solved, you become more aware of the others waiting beyond it - and also become better able to deal with them. The healing process is like peeling an onion, layer after layer. Only when one layer has been removed can you see what lies beneath it, until eventually you come to the core.

Don't worry if you feel let-down! Life issues are often identified and moved toward resolution in intensive healing sessions. This sometimes occurs through a process of stimulated memory-awakening (which may relate to the present and/or past lifetimes) and stirs up emotions which can be quite keenly felt.

After the intensity of accelerated self-healing, many people go through a let-down reaction in which they feel drained, uncertain or confused for a short time. This is a common pattern, and no cause for concern.

Don't hesitate to call for support! Some people go

through a denial phase, in which they retroactively reject the healing experience for a time or - rarely - altogether. Others experience short-term benefits, and then slip quietly into old patterns and old dis-eases. If you find yourself in denial or slippage, seek input and insight from those who are supporting your self-healing program.

Deal with your problems or challenges ***one at a time.*** Beginning by about the third or fourth day, your healing experience will leave you feeling renewed. You'll be more clear-headed and empowered; this is a good time to formulate plans and take action toward solving problems. Take one thing at a time, and deal with it. Then move on to the next challenge, and the next - with some rest and relaxation thrown in, for the sake of your physical, mental and spiritual well-being!

In most cases the physical disturbances associated with cleansing syndrome are relatively slight, and last for about 24 hours. In some instances, however, the release response can cause considerable discomfort including frequent urination, vomiting, diarrhea, profuse sweating, headaches, joint or muscle aches and pains, tearfulness, extreme fatigue, and so forth, and can continue for three days or at a diminished level of severity for as long as a week.

The Release of Dense Energies into a Refined Aura

Energy blockages occur as a result of retention or the unwillingness to experience the flow of negative or spent energies, which become lodged - and often tightly packed - in various body parts.

When these are released through Lightwork or bodywork into a "refined" aura - that is, the energy field of someone whose vibrational frequency has been and is rising at a significant pace toward fourth dimensional level - **the impact is accelerated and exaggerated.**

After you have dealt with all the major blockages and are well on the way toward full clarity, old emotional wounds may suddenly re-open and blocked energies that you were quite unaware of may manifest in attention-getting imbalances. These can hit you hard - not because they are inherently significant, but **because of the exaggerated impact of the release of dense blockages into the refined aura.**

This is one reason Lightworkers are so often in need of continuing self-healing. Other reasons have to do with their constant exposure to the negative energies of the world around them and their involvement in assisting the self-healing of others. Lightworkers are human: They need self-healing assistance, care and nurturing just like anyone else.

Use the Force! Universal energy is at your fingertips. Learn to accept this and align yourself with its flow, and you will never lack for strength.

The Universe supports your self-healing decisions. Learn to accept this, and the power of the Universe will flow more swiftly and smoothly in your body and in your life. After an assisted self-healing experience, **use the Force** to make your cleansing/release response a positive and uplifting process. Know that you are ridding your body of the accumulated blockages and toxins stored there over a long period of time.

Do your homework! Consider carefully the suggestions and follow-through instructions given by the professionals who are supporting your self-healing.

In regard to Healing Touch Therapy[1], the disavowals, affirmations and visualizations on your homework sheets are important to the embodiment of your self-healing decisions. It takes about 70 to 90 days to *embody* your decisions, i.e., to program them into the cellular memory of the body itself.

Say your disavowals and affirmations aloud, twice daily, for about 30 days. You may find that you adjust or amend them for maximum support, as you repeat them from day to day. After 30 days, you can do them three times a week for the remainder of the 90-day period.

If you are a Reiki practitioner, you may wish to say the disavowals and affirmations while giving yourself Reiki Light. Other less personalized affirmations for self-healing may also be used, such as:

I request perfect healing.
I request a perfect body.
I request perfect clarity of mind, (etc.)

Say each one three times.

Affirm the release-response as confirmation that healing has occurred.

The Universe supports your self-healing!

Chapter 10

TRANSCENDING TIME-LIMITATION AS AN EXERCISE IN SELF-HEALING

One of the parameters of third dimensional consensus reality is called ***time.*** The concept of linear earthplane "time" is a system of ordering experiences in sequence. One experience follows another in a sequence which is measured in seconds, minutes, hours, days, weeks, months, years, decades, centuries, millennia and so forth. The planet itself is patterned along seasonal and nocturnal/diurnal flow. For convenience, the time-concept is measured in direct relationship to the planetary flow-model.

You are now in an age of restructuring consensus reality from third dimensional vibrational frequency to fourth. Getting there from here is a process of overcoming limitations.

You begin stretching the boundaries of the possible, believing in the im-possible, practicing the im-possible - and making it work for you.

Learning to step in and out of the linear earthplane timeline at will is an excellent resource you can put to work in your life now. It also helps stretch your expectation of further non-limitation and helps you grow in self-chosen, intentionally applied personal empowerment. It's a vehicle you can use to explore your personal power.

Your self-healing process often includes meditations, affirmations, visualizations, energy exercises, and other methods of intentionally applying the focus of one's attention to the healing process. These are among the easiest tools to use in learning to move outside of earthplane time and use a "no-time" base for productive purpose.

You have already had no-time experiences, in the dream state. The content of a dream experience - what you perceived, what you felt, the sequence and intensity of dreamtime events, the personal evaluation of memory and meaning you retain after awakening - is in no way tied to the linear earthplane timeline. You can experience a vastly complex dream sequence in a matter of a few seconds that will take you hours to relate or write down.

The dream that takes no-time to happen takes hours to tell. Haven't you experienced this phenomenon?

Learning to consciously step in and out of no-time is an exercise in exploring altered states of consciousness - alternative dimensional realities - and using them productively. Time/no-time distinctions are akin to shamanic terminology, relating to ordinary reality and non-ordinary reality.

Working in a no-time base requires some preparation. Here's how to begin:

A. Choose an appropriate project and define it carefully. Your project must be SIGNIFICANT, SPECIFIC and MEASURABLE.

- To be SIGNIFICANT, it must have meaning to you.
- For it to be SPECIFIC, you have to define it in full detail.
- To make it MEASURABLE, you have to focus on a specified end result or other clear indication *in third dimensional physical consensus reality* that gives you evidence of the success or progress of the project. Otherwise you'll have no clear way of knowing whether it's working or not.

B. Visualize the whole process completely, in full detail, ***before*** you take it into no-time to put it into operation. Go over it again and again if need be, until it is completely clear in your mind's eye.

C. Consider the no-time entry, operation and return process. Make sure you understand it completely, so that you know where you are and what your options are at any point in the process.

Moving Into and Out of No-Time

The visualization itself is a very simple one:

See yourself entering a room full of timepieces of all sorts. There are grandfather clocks, mantel clocks, watches, alarm clocks, sundials, water clocks, time-keeping devices of every description that you can think of.

Look at the clocks. There is nothing else in the room. You are standing in the center of the room, looking at the time-keeping devices around you.

Notice how your body rhythms and life rhythms are correlated to *time.*

Say to yourself, **"I am in time."** Know it to be true. You are attuned to earthplane third dimensional linear timeline.

"I am in time."

Now see yourself walking across the room to a door on the opposite side. It doesn't matter where the door is, so long as it is a different one, not the same one through which you came into the room.

Reach out, open the door and step through it.

You now find yourself in a totally white space. There is no delineation between walls, floor, ceiling, yet you are not falling, you are standing comfortably on the white surface in the white space.

Now say to yourself, **"I am in no-time."**

Next you implement the pre-chosen program you have designed to be used in no-time by running through it verbally, and in visualization ***as fast as you can humanly say the words and see the fleeting images.***

As you continue to use no-time as a resource, you'll find you become more comfortable with the process. As it gets easier and more familiar to you, your speed in activating the program will naturally increase. There are also some additional short-cuts you can incorporate into the program, which will be given shortly.

As you near the end of your no-time program, begin slowing down the activation process. It is often helpful to finish up with a basic chakra-balancing exercise such as the stairstep or seawave sequences used as illustrations. (See below).

At the end of the program activation, take a deep breath ... relax ... you are in the totally white no-time space, approaching the door of the room of time.

Open the door of the room of time and step inside. Go to the center of the room and look at the clocks, all the timekeeping devices around you. Say to yourself, **"I am in time. I am in time."**

Consciously adjust your body rhythms to interact productively and comfortably with linear earthplane timeline, in your usual way.[15]

You may also wish to count yourself up from one to five, and say, *"Wide awake and feeling good."* Similar phrases and techniques for emerging from altered states of consciousness may also be used, of course.

Remember that your program has an element of success that can be *measured* by its effects upon the physical plane. As you emerge into time again, be observant. Notice how you feel, including any sensations that support your knowing something "really happened".

Exercise 1: Stairsteps (A Simple Energy-Balancing Exercise)

The *significance* of the program lies in its ability to balance body energies, through a visualization process using color visualization to activate the chakras.

In defining the program, take your time. Don't rush it. Make sure all details are clearly visualized and *felt*. Don't rush on to one part until the previous one feels complete to you.

Here is the exercise as it is *specifically defined*, in ordinary time:

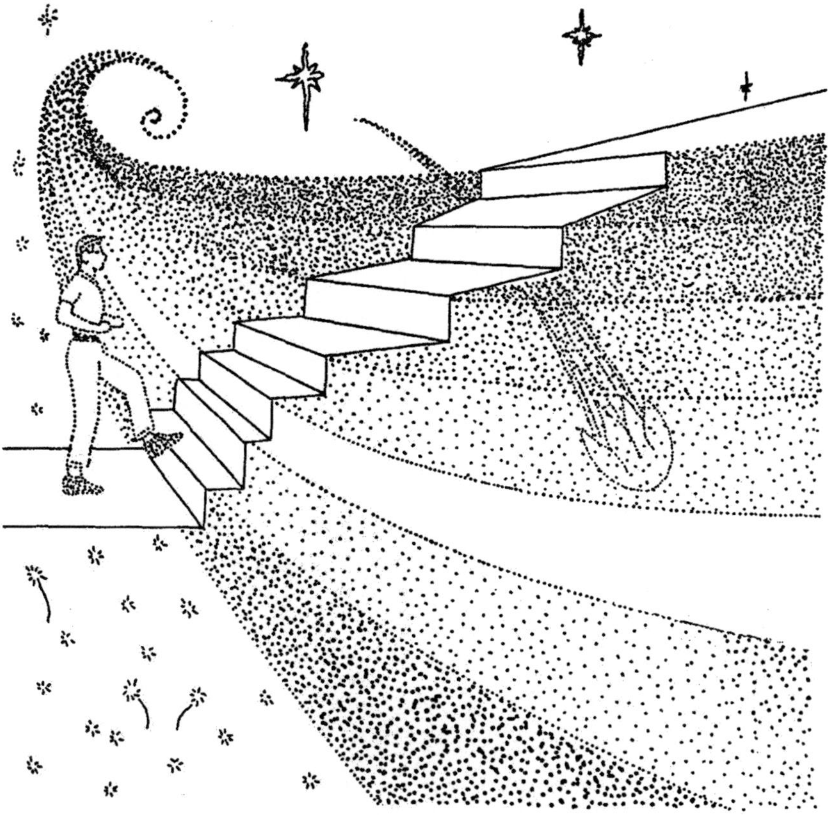

See before you a staircase. Walk toward it.

As you approach the first step, you see that it is a rich vibrant red color, flowing with sparkling crystal highlights ... a shimmering, flowing red ... beautiful ... rich

Put one foot on the red step and feel the richness of the red color begin to flow into your body ... bring your other foot onto the red step and let yourself be totally immersed in glorious vibrant red color; let it fill you completely ... stay until you are completely filled with beautiful rich red light ...

Now you see before you an orange step, flowing with brilliant crystal flecks of orange light ... admire the beauty of it. Move to the orange step, first one foot and then the other, and allow the vibrant orange light to come into your body, filling you completely ... luxuriate in the orange glow ... become at one with the orange light ...

Before you is a yellow step, sparkling with brilliant yellow colors ... swirling with yellow light ... enjoy its loveliness. Step onto the yellow step, first one foot and then the other, and let the warm rich yellow light fill you completely ... you are wonderfully, joyfully, peacefully, yellow ... let it soak into you. Let the yellow become a part of you ...

See before you a green step, marvelously glowing with green light ... let yourself want it ...yearn for it. Step up onto the green step, first one foot and then the other, and let the rich vibrant green color come into your body, filling you completely. Let it in! ... fill every nook and cranny of your being with joyful healing green light ... absorb it ...

In front of you is a blue step, twinkling with crystal highlights, beckoning ... see how beautiful and vibrant it is! Step up onto the blue step, first one foot and then the other, and let the glorious blue light come into your body ... clear sparkling blue, filling you completely ... become one with the blue light ...

Now before you there is an indigo step, deep and rich, glowing with promise ... admire it ... love it. Step up onto the indigo step, first one foot and then the other, and feel the rich indigo light flood into your being ... warm ... lovely ... deeply satisfying. Fill yourself completely with indigo light ...

See before you now the violet step, rich with depth and clarity of color lovelier than you ever before imagined. Step up onto the violet step, first one foot and then the other, and allow the violet light to come into your body ... feel it wash over you, richly satisfying ... deep vibrant color ... let it fill you completely ...

Before you now there is a white step, and you realize that is your destination, your goal. Look upon the clarity, the purity of the white step ... let yourself love it and yearn for it. Step up onto the white step, first one foot and then the other, and let the white light enter your body ... pure, rich, beautiful, satisfying ... balanced ... fill yourself with it completely ...

Take a deep breath. Relax. Don't rush.

Tune in to your body. Notice how you feel.

This energy-balancing exercise usually promotes a sense of relaxation, well-being, and balance. Minor aches and pains may have disappeared or lessened, and you will experience a sense of peace. Your response to the exercise is the *measurable* result the project has. This will be stronger in some persons than in others, especially the first few times you do the exercise.

People often experience increased color-visualization sensitivity through the practice of this exercise and similar programs.

The stairstep exercise usually takes anywhere from 5 to 15 minutes to complete. Now that it has been clearly defined in ordinary time, you can do the same exercise in no-time:

A. Choose the exercise, and have a clear understanding of its elements. You won't want to stop and wonder what comes next, once you're in no-time. Remind yourself of the measurable result you expect to feel, when the exercise has been completed.

B. See yourself going into the room of time, and through it into no-time. You are in no-time.

C. Run the program, by going over the key elements (say them aloud) and remembering the gist of the visualization they represent. Do this ***as fast as you can.***

Staircase ahead.
Red step ... two ... three.
Orange step ... two ... three.
Yellow step ... two ... three.
Green step ... two ... three.
Blue step ... two ... three.
Indigo step ... two ... three.
Violet step ... two ... three.
White step ... two ... three ...

D. Begin the re-entry into time process. (If this is the last or only program you are running in no-time, you start slowing the process down at the white step point.) Balancing ... balancing ... walk toward the door of the room of time ...

E. As you emerge into ordinary reality again, notice how you feel. When you have successfully completed the no-time process, you will have the same sensations as if you had done the whole visualization in ordinary time - only it will have taken just a few seconds, instead of several minutes!

Exercise 2: Seawave (Another Balancing Exercise)

First define the exercise in full detail, by going over it carefully in ordinary time.

In this exercise, we use the visualization of a sea of light, with waves of color rippling along its surface.

You lie upon the sand at its shore or float upon the waves effortlessly, in complete comfort and safety. One by one the waves of color flow over your entire body, from toe-tips to crown, filling you completely with each color in turn.

Here's what it looks like in no-time:

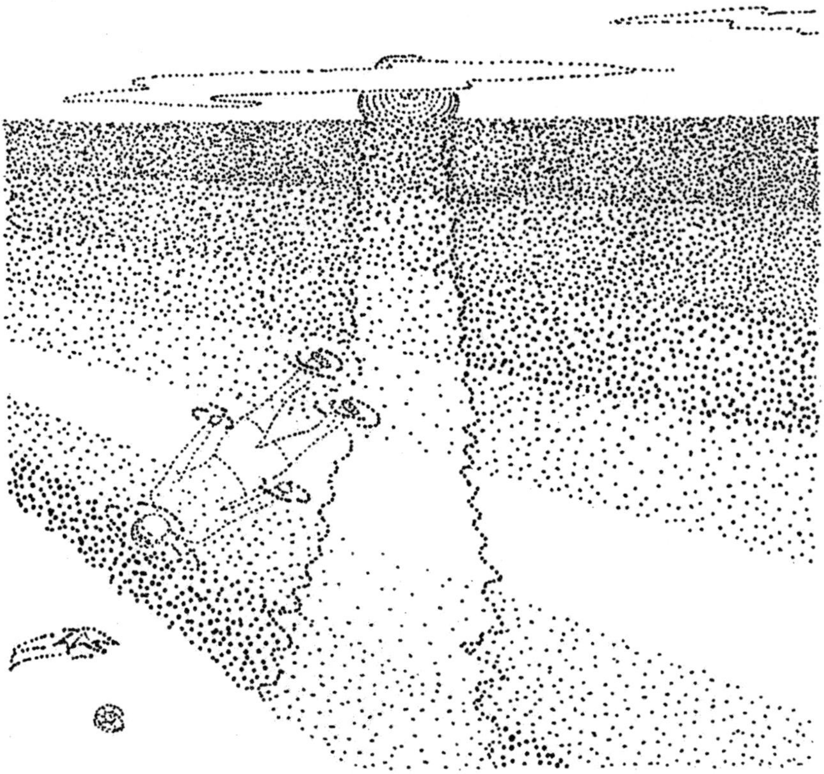

Room of time ... into no-time.
Red wave ... two ... three
Orange wave ... two ... three
Yellow wave ... two ... three
Green wave ... two ... three
Blue wave ... two ... three
Indigo wave ... two ... three
Violet wave ... two ... three
White wave ... (slowing down for re-entry) ... two ... three ...
Balancing ... balancing ...
Back into the room of time.
I am in time.
Adjust body rhythms to usual self-function.
One ... two ... three ... four ... five ...
Wide awake and feeling good.

There are any number of similar balancing exercises you can design for yourself. You might use colored balloons and bring them down over you, allowing them to burst and fill you with color. You could run from one color cloud to the next, or slide down each color-ray of the rainbow. Suit yourself! Be creative! **And remember to specifically design the program in full detail, before you take it into no-time.**

Exercise 3: Reike (Self-Healing in No-Time)

If you are a Reiki II practitioner or Reiki Master, you are familiar with the procedures for sending Reiki healing Light across time and space. These methods lend themselves readily to application in no-time.

Your no-time Reiki self-healing program might look something like this:

A. Choose the self-visualization *image* you will use. Picture yourself in a specific way, or use a photograph if this is helpful. You need not specify the place at which Light will be received, so long as time/purpose and image intentions are clearly stated and visualized.

B. Choose the *times* for reception of Reiki self-healing, i.e., 9:00, 10:00, 11:00, and so forth. One approach is to use each hour of the day for a 24-hour period, then do each day of the week.

C. Remind yourself clearly of the empowering symbols and their names. You should have them so firmly fixed in your mind's eye that when you say the symbol's name you will automatically get a visualization flash of it.

D. You may also wish to have a statement of healing intent or a series of such statements, to use along with the symbol name and visualization. Repeat each statement three times, to affirm your clear intent. Some popular ones are:

I choose perfect healing ...

I choose a perfect body ...
Every cell, every tissue, every organ ...

E. Turn on your hands, to awaken the healing Light and express your intention of bringing it through your body, flowing out the hands. In Reiki, this is done by visualization of specific symbols. You can do this either just before or just after you go into no-time.

F. Go into no-time, through the room of time.

G. To avoid the possible sudden onset of cleansing syndrome, state your intention that in any/every given hour, you will receive the Reiki in a balanced flow over the course of the entire hour, rather than in an abrupt intense beam that hits you every hour on the hour.[12]

Now run your pre-chosen program of giving yourself Reiki Light at specified intervals of time.

1:00 ... I choose perfect healing ... (repeat names of symbols used for distance healing.)
2:00 ... I choose perfect healing ... (repeat names)
3:00 ... I choose perfect healing ... (repeat names)
4:00 ... I choose perfect healing ... (repeat names)
5:00 ... I choose perfect healing ... (repeat names)
6:00 ... I choose perfect healing ... (repeat names)
etc.

Say the times, state your intention and repeat the symbols out loud or silently, as fast as you can.

H. When you have finished the program of giving yourself Reiki at specified times, you may want to do an energy-balancing exercise such as those given above, to prepare yourself for leaving no-time.

I. Balance out, start slowing down as you approach the door of the room of time, enter the room of time and exit from no-time into ordinary time using the methods previously given.

During this process you may extend your hands toward the

chosen self-image and feel the Reiki energy flow through your body, projected out your palms. You will probably notice that the sensations in your hands which are characteristic of taking-energy (as a cycle begins and flows) and not-taking-energy (as a cycle ends) alternate from one to the other very quickly. If this is confusing or distracting, you can just *visualize* your extended hands, instead of physically extending them.

Another way of using Reiki for self-healing in no-time is to use the symbols to empower a series of personal choices and requests. Instead of setting/using times or dates, you simply state your intention (while in no-time) and reinforce it by invoking Reiki Light with the appropriate symbol.

Here are some further examples:

I choose perfect health ...
I choose perfect function ...
Every cell, every tissue, every organ ...
I am strong and healthy ...
I am healing, I am healed ...
I am balanced, I am whole ...

You can also say, "*I request*" instead of or in addition to "*I choose*".

Another approach is to go through a listing of each body system, naming heart and circulatory system, spinal column and skeleton, lungs and respiratory system, etc. Here are more examples:

I request perfect teeth and gums ...
I request perfect hearing ...
I request perfect sight ...
I choose perfect strength ...
I choose a perfect weight ...
I choose a perfect digestion ...
I choose a perfect metabolism ...
I choose mental clarity ...
I choose excellent memory ...
I choose emotional stability ...
I choose emotional healing ...

I choose mental health ...
I choose abundance ...
I choose financial healing ...
I choose action toward success in my career ...
I choose spontaneous right action ...

The list is potentially endless. Use your imagination!

The results of giving yourself Reiki healing in no-time will be about the same as giving yourself Reiki in ordinary time. It just won't take you as long to do it!

There are two primary ways to do Reiki (or other) self-healing programs in no-time. The first is to select a specific set of goals and focus on them intently. The second is to take advantage of what would otherwise be an unproductive use of time - such as in waiting rooms, on long drives, and at other moments of opportunity for purely mental/spiritual focus. When you are frustrated at not being able to take action on the physical level, you can seize the moment and do something active on the metaphysical levels.

The more you use no-time, the easier it gets. After a little practice, you can slip in and out almost anytime, anywhere, without people around you being any the wiser.

There are a number of other ways of learning to transcend the limitations of third dimensional linear timeline. You can also use a combination of methods to create even stronger programs. For example, you can combine no-time with the use of personally created/empower rituals, or "macros".

Macros:
Creating and Empowering Personal Rituals

Words have power.
As you speak it, so shall it be unto you.
Be careful what you ask for. You might get it.
If you can dream it, you can do it.

Words have power. Where does that power come from?

Words have the power *you give them.* Words communicate thought. They embody images, concepts and intentions. They are expressions of your personally created reality and your intention for the creation of personal reality.

The reality of the family is created by images, concepts and intentions expressed - by words, and by other means - within the family. The reality of a tribe or ethnic constituency is created by and embodied in its language and customs. Belief and behavioral systems are described as cultural *monads*, expressed and embodied in the words used to describe them and the actions used to practice them.

Words and gestures often have both primary and secondary meanings. The interpersonal reality of a society or a nation is created by and embodied in its language and customs, including slang usage and the fashion of the moment.

Words are powerful. Even in ordinary everyday use, they automatically convey a message to others, to the Universe, and even to yourself. Habitual right choice of words and concepts promotes self-healing and self-realization; habitual use of negative words and concepts can be toxic.

Words can also be consciously used to create ritually empowered tools for personal transformation, such as those we call "macros".

In computer terminology, a "macro" is a code key sequence designed to set a series of predetermined choices into active motion.

Just entering a macro key sequence won't set anything into motion unless you - or someone else - have planned and *programmed* (i.e., chosen) something. The macro is just the command code that activates your pre-designed sequence of choices.

Similarly, a word doesn't become a ritually empowered tool until you or someone else has defined the ritual it is intended to embody.

The word "amen" is a good example of ritual empowerment. It has long been used as an expression of agreement. Saying "amen" at the end of a prayer is a personal affirmation of the prayer. Saying "amen" in casual conversation means, "I emphatically agree with you."

In a similar vein, the sign of the cross is a ritually empowered symbolic action commonly used in many Christian traditions, often accompanied by the ritually empowered words "In the name of the Father, and of the Son, and of the Holy Spirit. Amen."

In other traditions of faith, there are equally evocative ritual words and symbols. Salaam ... Shalom ... Namaste'... the Wai ... Blessed Be ... All our relations, All our relations ... Ho! - the list is endless.

These are powerful ritual words and symbols because they have been *empowered* by common use, for hundreds of years. Somebody invented, defined and began to use them. Others learned, adopted, and sometimes redefined or amended them. With every intentional use, they became more and more empowered. You share with others in their use, which is commonly held.

You can also create and empower *personal* rituals, for your own private use. You can set up your own programs, and embody them in your own macro designations.

The first step is simple: Choose a program. Design and define it carefully, in every detail. Once your details are clear, break down the process into several segments. These can be labeled A, B, C, and so forth, or 1, 2, 3, whatever you prefer.

So long as there is no inherently negative connotation to them (i.e., death, pain, famine, hell) the labels themselves don't matter. You can call your segments mayonnaise, mustard, catsup and pickle - whatever you wish.

Next, choose a name for the overall macro. This is the word you will empower and use to activate the program. Again, it can be any word or word combination you choose - but avoid the negatives, please! If you use words with negative connotations, they'll come back to haunt you sooner or later.

To *use* the macro, after it has been designed and named, we recommend a command code such as "Macro-name, activate now" or "Macro-name, execute *now.*" This will prevent unintentional accidental activation of the program.

For example, you may have chosen an innocent word such as "broccoli" for your macro's name. You don't want to have the program activated every time you say "Would you care for some broccoli?" or someone says it to you!

To illustrate the process, we choose the macro designation: Cocoon.

MACRO EXERCISE 1: COCOON
(A Protection Ritual For Automobile Travel)

Part A: (accompanied by the appropriate visualization)

To the North, to the South,
To the East, to the West,
To the Northwest, to the Southwest,
To the Northeast, to the Southeast,
Above me, below me,
Before me, behind me,
To my right, to my left,
To my right rear quarter, to my right front quarter,
To my left rear quarter, to my left front quarter,

Part B: (visualizing along with the words)

Cocoon of Light.
Cocoon, cocoon, cocoon.
Cocoon, cocoon, cocoon.
Safety, Safety, Safety.
Safety, Safety, Safety.
No ticket, no ticket, no ticket.
No ticket, no ticket, no ticket.
No car trouble, no car trouble, no car trouble.
No car trouble, no car trouble, no car trouble.
Safety, Safety, Safety.
Safety, Safety, Safety.
Speed. (This part is optional!)

Part C: (Extension)

Cocoon, Cocoon, Cocoon.
Cocoons of Light for me and mine.
(Visualize each one of the family cars, or the other cars you wish to include in this protective ritual.)
Cocoon (name the make and year of car you're riding in)
Cocoon (name the make and year of other car(s) in turn).
Safety, Safety, Safety.

Now we have a three-part macro named Cocoon. You begin by using it this way:

Part A:

To the North, to the South
To the East, to the West
To the Northwest, to the Southwest,
To the Northeast, to the Southeast,
Above me, below me,
Before me, behind me,
To my right, to my left,
To my right rear quarter, to my right front quarter,
To my left rear quarter, to my left front quarter,

Cocoon, Part B, activate NOW.

Part C:

Cocoon, Cocoon, Cocoon.
Cocoons of Light for me and mine.
(Visualize each one of the family cars, or the other cars you wish to include in this protective ritual.)
Cocoon (name the make and year of car you're riding in)
Cocoon (name the make and year of other car(s) in turn).
Safety, Safety, Safety.

Segmenting the program into parts and moving by degrees into a ritually empowered macro is a lead-in technique to familiarize yourself with the process of creating macros. It also aids in assuring clarity of detail, especially in the more complex rituals. The next step is obvious:

Cocoon, activate *NOW*.

There are many potential variations on the theme:

Cocoon, *re*-activate NOW. (After a stop for gas or meals)
Cocoon, reinforce *NOW*. (You just saw a police car and don't know how fast you were going, or you otherwise feel threatened in some way.)

Cocoon, this plane, NOW. (You're traveling by air this time, and not using a separate ritual for air travel.)

Personal Cocoon, max-strength, *NOW*. (You're afoot and feel nervous or threatened.)

Remember: Using empowered macros to embody your personal rituals is based on the principle of your stated personal intention, backed by your personal power. It's mainly a time saver. If your macro has been carefully crafted and empowered, it will be exactly as strong as the long-form ritual would be - no more and no less.

Prayers, mantras, affirmations, visualizations and other tools for personal or interpersonal transformation can be embodied into empowered macros. Once you have developed them carefully to express your true intentions, you can use the no-time and macro shortcut methods to support any interpersonal, society or planetary energy shift focus you espouse.

For instance, you can participate in Prayer for Peace, Earth Day, World Peace Day, Divine Mercy, or any other movement through direct energy flow generated by your intentional positive use of no-time meditations and macros - all without increasing the amount of linear time you spend focusing on them!

Participating in this way will enhance, rather than replace, the way you give, receive and focus group energy at a gathering.

What other potential use can you make of these metaphysical time-saving techniques? Use your imagination!

Like any other rituals, macros tend to increase in strength with frequent intentional use. Repetition builds power.

It takes 70 to 90 days to *embody* a change. Personal decisions (old and new) are stored in the cellular memory of the body, where they continue to operate as "default settings" until and unless you do something intentional to change them.

Therefore, when you embark on an intentional program of self-healing, meditation or manifestation you should stick with it diligently for at least 90 days. Don't become discouraged or distracted too easily - and don't give up too soon.

One of the main reasons people fail to realize their self-healing, self-exploration or manifestation goals is that they don't stay with the program long enough to make it work. It's true that the time required for full impact varies from one individual to another. It's also true that it takes 70 to 90 days for most people's *bodies* to get the message about decisions their minds have made.

Once a decision is firmly encoded in cellular memory, it becomes a working pattern that is relatively easy to maintain.

Setting new habits requires persistence! The no-time and macro concepts give you a means of sticking with your program persistently and consistently, with relatively little clock-time spent on them.

You can use macros in either ordinary time or no-time.

Time-Warps and Space-Warps

Time and space warps are related. They both have to do with how long it takes you to get where you want to go, or how long it takes you to do what you want to do.

Have you ever noticed that sometimes time flies and sometimes it crawls? Your *feeling* about the passage of time is based on the way in which you personally interact with the third dimensional linear timeline. Change your *intention* of how you experience the timeline, and you will change your reality.

Once you get the hang of it, changing the pace of your interaction with the linear timeline is no more difficult than changing the setting on a metronome. You can program slow-down settings for some activities and speed-up settings for others.

You don't have to leave the metronome on the same setting all day, or all your life. You can change it! And when you become more adept at managing two or more dimensional realities simultaneously, you can run slow programs on one level and fast levels on another!

The possibilities are limitless. And that's the point: this is the age of transition, the age in which you learn to overcome limitations.

Some time/space warps are easier to manage when you're doing and/or thinking about something else. Intense focus - including that which is called "living in the now", or "conscious living" - tends to lock you into the linear timeline limitation which is still a prevailing condition of third dimensional earthplanet reality.

The best way to step outside linear time/space and still practice living in the now is to go to a simultaneous multidimensional personal consciousness system. Learning this won't really do you any good unless you are truly maintaining conscious living on a regular basis, clear of any major personal blockages and otherwise ready for the more complex approach.

Here are some general tips about working with time/space warps:

- You are less likely to manifest a successful warp when frustrated, angry, fearful or otherwise immersed in a negative personal energy situation.
- If you want a warp, you can't keep watching the clock. A watched pot never boils!
- People who stay rigidly tuned in to their immediate surroundings are less likely to get a good warp than those who allow their minds to wander.
- Because the "prove it to me" syndrome can be a strongly counterproductive factor, you're less likely to get a warp when you're watching for it than when you aren't. If you don't allow yourself to believe it can happen, it won't.
- If you get a good warp and explain it away by assuming you've misread the clock or miscalculated in some way, you are rejecting the principle of transcending limitations. Some people do this consistently: miracles occur and are denied, explained away. And unless you adjust your conscious thought patterns to be more open, it will be just that much harder for you to break through the barrier next time.

Unless you are using music as (a) a return-focus device - as one might when doing out of body travel in no-time or non-sleep dreamtime, for example - or (b) background noise to distract and lull the overly active conscious brain-chatter, it is likely to interfere with your warp.

Music is timeline-keyed, and your body/mind rhythms tend

to synchronize with it. If you use music, you will need to specify (by stating your intention) that the music is to key itself to your rhythm, and not vice versa. Some tape players are more capable of permitting this than others. Older models are not recommended.

A long highway drive is an excellent opportunity for exploring time/space warp capability. Begin by expressing your intention.

IMPORTANT!! WARNING!! Most people are capable of a sort of "automatic" driving, especially on familiar streets and highways, which allows the attention to wander without endangerment. If you aren't comfortable doing that; if you have a tendency to become a less capable and careful driver when your attention wanders, then DO NOT PRACTICE TIME/SPACE WARP EXPERIMENTS WHILE OPERATING A MOTOR VEHICLE OR ANY POTENTIALLY DANGEROUS PIECE OF EQUIPMENT OR MACHINERY. Use your common sense! Know yourself!

If your automatic situational response reflexes are poor, you are relying mainly on conscious focus (rather than unconscious reflex) to maintain personal safety and wellbeing. In that case, time/space warp driving is not for you! If you want to experiment with transcending time/space limitation, do it in some *other* context.

When you make the decision to go for a time/space warp, what are you saying? Think about it.

You are saying to yourself and to the Universe:

"I do not choose to limit myself and my actions to the parameters defined as linear earthplane timeflow."

"I choose to step outside the rules-of-the-game called third dimensional reality."

"I slough off the bonds of time. I create my own timeless spaceless reality, according to my own needs and choices."

State your intention aloud. Make it clear in your own mind.

Your goals should be well defined, as in other metaphysical exercises, but much more flexible. Define a specific goal or expectation, such as cutting an hour's travel time off a six-hour trip *without increasing driving speed, skipping a usual stop, or otherwise altering your usual travel pattern.*

Then give yourself some slack: Don't consider the experiment a failure if you only cut 45 minutes off the trip, or even half an hour. The goal must be measurable, so you'll have some way of gauging your results, but not rigid.

Know what time you leave home. After that, *don't watch the clock!* If you happen to catch a glimpse of a timepiece inadvertently, just don't tune in to it.

Don't calculate time-and-mileage segments.

Don't watch the odometer or the highway mile-markers.

***DO** watch your speedometer, and maintain your usual driving speed.*

It's usually best not to start a serious exploration of time/space warp drivetime when you're running late and worried about making up time. It can be done - especially by those who are already adept at it - but it's often counterproductive to fail to allow yourself adequate driving time and count on getting a warp.

You don't want to be nervous and frustrated about the process. Be easy-going and just let it flow.

In fiction and especially in science fiction (and in some very concrete, very tangible physical experiments such as the Philadelphia incident as well), the concept of transcending the timeline limitation has most commonly explored in terms of **time-travel** or **time-stasis devices** (i.e., H. G. Wells' *The Time Machine*, John D. MacDonald's *The Girl, The Gold Watch and Everything)* or in terms of trans-temporal and/or trans-spacial **telekinetic ability** (as in Anne McCaffrey's *Pegasus Flight* and *The Rowan).*

Some researchers are currently working on developing and perfecting time-devices. These tend to be highly specialized projects not available to the general public, while the direct metaphysical approach is something anyone can learn and take. You are learning to use an applied combination of personal energy and Universal energy to re-shape not only your personal realities but the reality of the earthplanet as a whole.

Someone has to lead. Why not you? Your own inner

guidance will tell you whether a focus on transcending third dimensional time/space limitation is appropriate for your immediate agenda.

In principle, ***any* successful experiments in transcending third dimensional consensus reality limitations contribute to your self-healing and the healing of the planet.**

If you can dream it, you can do it. Weeding the word "impossible" out of your internal vocabulary is important. It prepares you to meet new challenges with confidence; to achieve and maintain overall a balanced state of body, mind and spirit wellness no matter what the tasks of the moment may demand of you.

The 1990s are and will be wonderful! And they are and will be challenging. Those who are most fully prepared to meet the challenges with confidence will be best able to appreciate the wonders.

Healing is also a *completion:* the third dimensional phase of this planet's development is being healed - completed - through a process loosely called ***the manifestation of mass consciousness: implementation of the new fourth dimensional consensus reality.*** You are very much a part of this. Every personal self-healing achievement contributes to the healing of the planet as a whole.

Healing At A Distance

With the exception of direct bodywork (massage therapy, chiropractic manipulation, etc.) or the use of physical tools or objects (i.e., magnetic wellness support products, some psychotronic devices, substances directly applied to or ingested into the body, etc.) almost any method successfully used for in-person healing can also be used for healing at a distance.

Reiki, Mahikari and several other methods of natural healing teach procedures for healing at a distance. Native American and other shamanic traditions also commonly feature distance healing, as do prayer healing, meditation circles, psychological and psychospiritual counseling (which can readily be conducted by telephone, and often have a strong healing support impact), and many other disciplines or practices.

Healing at a distance can be conducted by individuals

and/or by groups. Distance healing can be focused on individuals, groups, societies, species, situations, or the planet as a whole. And like any other form of healing, the strength of its impact depends largely on the person or group of persons participating. Some people are stronger at it than others.

A pure heart and true desire to help are often more important than technical know-how.

Many self-healing support practitioners offer distance healing as a professional service. It is well to remember that there must be an exchange of energy in any venture for it to be fully productive. The laborer is worthy of his hire and deserves to be honored and supported in his work. And those who receive professional healing service without compensating the healer often undervalue and reject the gift.

When you accept an idea, you often say, "I'll buy that!" The opposite is also often true: if you "buy" something, with money or other exchange value, you are more likely to accept it and use it. If you don't "buy" it, i.e., don't pay for it, you don't accept it.

Chapter 11

WHAT DOES EARTH-HEALING HAVE TO DO WITH YOU?

You are in the process of redefining your self-chosen individual roles in the life of the earthplanet and the life of the Universe. You are remembering the infinite beginnings of your Be-ingness. You are once again become co-creators of your own life and the life of the society and reality in which you live.

You are accepting responsibility for your life and for the life of your society, your planet, your reality ... your Universe.

You are embracing your lessons, knowing you have chosen to learn them. Instead of looking for someone to blame for the challenges in your life, you are seeking higher meaning in them - and resourceful ways to meet them effectively, joyfully!

These are acts of personal growth, personal healing. These are acts of earth growth, earth healing. The more you experience healing and balance in your own life, the more eager you are to share information and experience with others. As you become more and more free of personal lessons, personal blockages, personal limitations, personal distractions, you become more and more able - and willing - to involve yourself in supporting the healing of others and the healing of the planet.

You awaken to *your* potential for manifesting mass consciousness. You become a more consciously interactive part of the whole.

All healing is earth-healing. When you heal yourself and support others in their self-healing, you also assist in the healing of the planet. This is our goal, shared by persons of goodwill (whether incarnate or discarnate) throughout the earth and throughout the Universe.

The positive Universe supports the healing of planet earth. The positive Universe supports *your* self-healing and the healing of other individuals, as a personalized manifestation of planetary healing.

Planetary Health Concerns: Only YOU Can Heal the Earth

Smokey Bear says, "Only **you** can prevent forest fires." Conscious choice on the part of the individual (you) for responsible behavior (rejecting those actions likely to create forest fires) is necessary to assure the desired common-benefit goal (preservation of forests).

Only you can heal the earth. The choice begins in your own heart and thoughts, and is implemented by your own actions.

The earth-healing process begins with your personal self-healing. You cannot reach full potential in supporting the healing of others - or the planet - without commitment to that personal state of wellness/balance which is your self-chosen goal for this moment of your life/growthpath.

Earth-healing begins with self-healing. This point must be repeated over and over again, to overcome the commonly-held perception that it is somehow "selfish" to focus on self-care and self-realization.

Through many ages past, you have been taught that service to others comes through a willingness to sacrifice yourself. Although that concept had merit in its own time, in its own ways, it is not fully appropriate for the age in which you now live.

The intent behind the injunction toward willingness to sacrifice oneself on behalf of others was to acknowledge that (as Mr. Spock says) the needs of the many outweigh the needs of the few, or the one. It was a recognition of collective need for health/balance; a stimulus toward a less limited, less myopic view of personal reality.

This excellent principle, however, has often come to be interpreted as an injunction toward consistently setting aside one's own needs in favor of those of other individuals or constituencies, without a true regard for whether the impact of that action will benefit the *whole.*

In your modern society, the needs and rights of persons/constituencies are in conflict with those of other persons/constituencies on a constant basis. The decisionmaking process of the judicial system and other governmental agencies has come to mean adjudicating between one set of personal/constituency rights and another, without regard for the rights or needs of the whole. In America, you go to great lengths to promote the public perception of "equality".

Certainly, all humans are gifted of GodForce with equal opportunity to live, learn and grow. Each spiritual Be-ing chooses for himself/herself that personal collection of challenges, opportunities, lessons and accomplishments that suit her/his personal needs. It is a noble thing for a person or a nation to be dedicated toward providing the optimum climate in which free will, self-chosen, can manifest itself.

Yet how does partial or complete anarchy (lack of government; lack of order) provide true freedom of choice for those whose self-adopted lifestyle need is for a more gentle and less aggressive existence than that of their neighbor?

Does not the over-reliance on the *physical* aspect of "survival of the fittest" constitute an evolutionary step backward on humanity's lifepath? Are not the qualities of wisdom, discretion, creativity and cooperative interaction also survival and growth tools?

At its best, government is the action arm of community. Community is interaction between individuals. Interaction at personal, group, societal, national, international, interspecie and cosmic levels is the vehicle for moving from individual consciousness to Universal consciousness. It is growth, which is the inherent goal of all Be-ings.

Are all persons' choices and lifestyles of equal value in terms of their contribution to mass consciousness, the corporate choice of the whole? Are all persons' choices equally wise? Are they equally conducive to their own growth and supportive of the growth of others?

Are all persons' choices equally supportive of the common peace, the common tranquility, the common good?

Over-controlling, as a general practice, does not support the needs of planetary growth. Over-controlling is an expression of power-over. *Under*-controlling also does not support the needs of planetary growth. It is an expression of lack of order and direction.

Balance is the answer. The serving of mutually-chosen, mutually-affirmed need - "mass consciousness" - is the answer.

At higher levels of understanding and higher dimensional vibrational frequencies, there is no conflict between individual "rights" and the needs of the whole. Beyond blockages and lessons, beyond the conflictive principles of power-over (whether expressed by individuals, groups, societies, governments) there is the principle of cooperatively expressed power-within.

Government of the people by the people, for the people ... joining together for the common good, while affirming the highest possible degree of freedom for individual choice, individual expression of Be-ingness in all its glorious complexity.

That which truly harms the whole cannot benefit the individual. That which truly harms the individual cannot ultimately benefit the whole.

That which is truly beneficial to the individual benefits the whole.

The concept of self-sacrifice as a vehicle for achieving spiritual growth is another of the limitations you are in the process of overcoming, in this age of transition.

This does not mean that serving the needs of others is unspiritual. Service to others and to the Universe is an expression of the need for fulfillment and satisfaction of your own Higher Self. It is the *sacrificial* aspect - setting your own needs aside; failing to nurture and care for yourself - which creates a counterproductive imbalance.

Bringing yourself low to serve the needs of others or the whole will not accomplish that purpose, because it is clearly an imbalance.

From time to time there are instances in which short-term personal needs are set aside in order to meet the urgent needs of others; yet self-sacrifice on a long-term or generalized basis isn't productive.

The concept of self-sacrifice is essentially regressive, based on scarcity-consciousness. Self-empowerment and self-affirmation are tools of growth/realization/healing in the present age. Seeing oneself as but a minute part of the organism of the whole often mistakenly supports the theory of self-sacrifice, lack of self-significance.

For optimum effect in supporting self-healing and its consequent earth-healing impact, the opposite approach is required.

The first law of healing is to heal yourself, first. You must acknowledge your own worth before you can truly acknowledge the worth of others. You must acknowledge your own power, before you can truly acknowledge the power of others.

You are a powerful being. Know this, and you prepare yourself to support the self-empowerment of others.

Tips For Interactive Planetary Self-Care

You are becoming more and more aware of the ways in which your personal wellness and self-created personal reality have an impact on planetary wellness and co-created planetary reality.

It's an exciting age in which to live! By your personal choices and interactive personal co-creative power you are bringing about major shifts in mass consciousness through personal example, teaching, and even through various metaphysical practices of shifting energies to harness the Universal LifeForce toward a swifter creation of the new realities. Like the earthplanet itself, you are coming of age!

Among the numerous hallmarks of your personal and planetary growing up process are an increase in your perceived need for clearing group blockages (as well as personal ones) and an increased desire to connect with others in support of mutual growth, mutual goals. You instinctively know there is a synergistic impact when personal power and intention are joined into *group* power and intention.

As you gather for *any* purpose, with persons of similar vibrational frequency and intent for good, a joined energy is formed which automatically supports the goals you jointly hold ... such as world peace, sound ecological and conservation practices, sending Light to any common focus, for the highest common good. Even if you are playing cards, drinking beer and swapping jokes, the gathering of your energies is an effective force for healing and growth.

> If your gathering generates positive energy, positive energy will not only fill each one of you, it will flow out to the whole world.

If your gathering generates negative energy, negative energy will fill each one of you, and will flow out to the whole world.

If your gathering is without focus, the energy will flow - without clearly directed focus.

When you focus the energy intentionally, it flows swiftly and surely to the focus you have chosen.

Gathering creates group-energy on an exponential, rather than a linear, progression base. Instead of 1 + 1 + 1 + 1, it is multiplied and remultiplied by the number of persons in the group. For example, if there are three of you it would be 3 x 3 = 9; 9 x 9 = 81; and so forth. If there are 10 of you, it goes 10 x 10 = 100; 100 x 100 = 10,000; 10,000 x 10,000 = 100,000,000; and so forth.

THIS IS HOW MASS CONSCIOUSNESS IS MANIFESTED.

It only takes about two percent of the population base to effectively change the reality of the whole.

You can take another step up in power-flow impact by adding conscious intent. *Focus.* When your group chooses a goal and intentionally focuses on it, the results are even more powerful than the simple gathering has already produced.

When you intentionally "send Light", waves of Light flow out from the power center you have created.

How To Focus Group Intention and Send Light: Understanding and Creating Ceremony

What tool do you use to express co-creator intent to change or otherwise define your chosen reality? *Energy.* Like ritual words and phrases, mantras and mandalas, dancing and singing, **ceremonies are expressions of energy.**

Every ceremony is newly created and unique in and of itself. It is composed of the energy expression, co-creatively expressed by the people who participate in it. You can create personal ceremonies all your own, and you can participate in co-created ceremonies with any number of others.

Although each ceremony is created afresh during its performance, by the personal and/or collective energy it expresses, many ceremonies are formatted along established lines of intention-flow. This builds added energy - power - by drawing upon the intentional energy expressions of those who initially designed the format, those who adapted it from time to time and expressed it in new ways, and those who have used it over the years.

The celebration of the Mass, in Roman Catholic tradition, is a good example of a ceremonial format which has been *empowered by intentional focus and further empowered by common usage.* Yet each celebration, each ceremony is newly co-created by the participants. Ceremony is an expression of energy, and the energy has never been expressed in exactly this way before.

Every ceremony, no matter how time-honored its origins and no matter how widely it is practiced, is a newly co-created expression of energy. The words and gestures may be the same; the format may be the same; the people present may even be the same - and the energy expressed by the ceremony has never been exactly the same before, and will never be exactly the same again.

Ceremonies - expressions of energy - which lack a clear intentional focus will be less powerful than those that have it.

Ceremonies with a high level of negative energy in them, unconsciously shared by those present who are feeling negative thoughts or emotions, will be less powerful than those in which high levels of positive or clear energy are generated by individual participants. It's your party; you can cry if you want to.

Ceremonies which invite and invoke the present of higher powers are more powerful than those that do not.

Ceremonies that are practiced in a pre-existing format that has traditionally been used in positive ways, to express positive intention, are more likely to be powerful in positive ways. You are building on the intentionally positive foundation of the past.

Ceremonies that are practiced in a pre-existing format which has traditionally been used in negative ways, to express negative intention, are less likely to be powerful in positive ways - *even when they are conducted with a positive intent focus.* You are setting yourself to overcome the negative foundation of the past.

The ceremonial use of negative energy is not as prevalent as it once was in earthplane usage, yet it is still known and feared in many societies. The ritualized *ceremonial* use of negative energy, which sometimes includes group focus and/or the invocation of negative energy based power figures, is more powerful than the casual (and often unintentionally expressed) *personal* use of negative energy or words. For example: ritually/ceremonially applied curses and spells are more likely to be more powerful than saying, "Damn him!." (Especially if you didn't really mean to damn him.)

When we are speaking of spells and curses, it's important to note the intended recipient doesn't have to accept the negative energy package that is directed to her or him. It can be rejected intentionally or automatically, by a variety of methods. The simplest is non-belief. It takes an extremely strong level of negative energy, intentionally directed, to get through to a person who doesn't believe in spells and curses.

The Master Teacher you call the Christ was one who led you away from the ceremonial use of negative energy. Even with regard to personal matters, he advised you to "forgive your enemies, and pray for those who spitefully use you." That was a powerful statement against holding/using negative energy focus, and a giant step forward toward a higher level of understanding in the use of positive and negative energy flow patterns.

The Buddha advocated the principle of Ahimsa - harm toward none - and practice of the Middle Way, a balanced approach to life. That, too, was a powerful step forward in understanding and using positive and negative energy flow patterns.

The various teachings of many other Masters and Avatars can be also interpreted in this way, as they relate to teaching the principles of positive and negative energy flow patterns. And even your modern sayings: "What goes around comes around."

Ceremonies - expressions of energy - that are in a language base that reflects the basic concept of power-over are not as powerful as ceremonies in a language base that affirms the basic concept of power-within.

This is an important point which many of you have not yet recognized: it is more powerful and productive to say, "God, I know you will support me in helping myself" than it is to say "God, please help me."

Which statement is based on the power-within concept?

Which statement is based on the power-over concept?

The concept of power-over is not limited to a negative context. It also applies to positive power-over situations, i.e., "Thou art great and I am small."

Think of the old hymn, "Trust and Obey ... there's no other way." It is an example of the many hymns and liturgical materials which are falling out of favor and usage in many Christian congregations. Those who affirm the miracles of the future, rather than seeking to preserve the limitations of the past, are focused on moving from a power-over language base to one that affirms power-within.

Moving from a power-over language base to a power-within language base in your communication with the Universe (God, the All, by whatever names have meaning for you) does not deny God's power or imply a lack of respect. It affirms your confidence in your interactive co-creative partnership with God. You take responsibility for your choices, and become conscious of your central role as co-creator of your personal and corporate realities.

When you begin to become one with God, accepting the Life-Force of the Universe as a very present, active and powerful aspect of your own Be-ing, you open the way for the whole range of creative acts we call "miracles".

Here is a way you can state your intention to move toward Oneness with God: If in your mind's eye and heart of hearts you envision God as a personal figure, step up ... take God's hand in yours, and say, *"You are in my heart. I am in your heart. I know that we are One."*

If the EarthMother/the Goddess is your focal point figure of faith, see her in your mind's eye. Go to her ... let her embrace you ... feel her love. *"You are in my heart. I am in your heart. I know that we are One."*

This visualization process can be used with any appropriate figure of faith. You needn't even limit yourself to one - choose several! Let them come into your heart ... feel their love. Let it heal you. Ask their help in right use of will, toward healing others. Ask their help in right use of will, toward healing the earthplanet.

We are coming back together, becoming One. Our ceremonies - expressions of energy - reflect this knowledge, which ultimately wells up from within every heart and every higher self.

Some Useful Ceremonial Formats: Opening and Closing Circles

Many gatherings begin and/or close with a circle of sharing. In the Native American tradition, there is a sacred circle and an invocation of Spirit presences. Dancing is a part of many ceremonies. Some excellent insights into the Native American (and other) ceremonial format are given in *American Indian Magic*, by Brad Steiger.

Ceremonial circles can be boundaried by stones or crystals, drawn in the sand, ringed with cleansing fire, chalked on the floor, or just loosely formed by a circle of people holding hands. It's your ceremony - you can dress it up or wing it; anything you like!

Here are some helpful hints:

- When you do an outdoor ceremony, it is a courtesy to make a greeting and ritual gift offering to the spirits of the land and the ancients in that place.
- Tobacco is one such ritual gift traditionally used in North America. Take a pinch and place it on the earth or throw it in the air, at the four cardinal directions of the compass. Small crystals are also highly effective because they are universally recognized as a gift to the earth, a giving something back, and because they are energy tools.
- In a dry land, a small pouring out of water is appropriate. You can also simply "give energy", by filling yourself with Universal LifeForce from the cosmos, which you then give to the earth by placing your hands on the ground.
- Any ceremony that has to do with the earth will be facilitated by taking off your shoes, nylons (especially nylons!), or other items of clothing that are not made of natural fibers. The energy does not flow smoothly through clothing that is produced through chemical technology. If you are in a high-energy situation (either personally or in a group), you're more likely to get overheated or otherwise uncomfortable if wearing synthetic fibers. In fact, you can even get energy-burn spots on your skin, similar to sunburn.
- If you are indoors, you way wish to connect your ceremony

to the earth itself by visualization and conscious grounding. In your mind's eye, see yourself growing roots. See your feet sprouting roots from the foot chakra (at the arch of the foot) which grow swiftly, deeply, through any intervening carpet, flooring, lower floors of the structure in which you are standing, through the foundations, topsoil, subsoil, into the very heart of the earth itself. Make sure you get past the crust, all the way to the magma level. Visualize the fiery rich molten flow; the life-stuff of the planet's inner reaches.

- Choose a leader to assist in focusing the intention of the circle, by her or his words and personal energy. If it's your circle, you are the leader - unless you select and designate someone else to fill that role.

  It is helpful to have a leader who is knowledgeable and articulate. It is also well to remember that a good heart and good energy are more powerful than empty words (those without positive energy behind them). If the leader has a high level of personal credibility with the group, so much the better. That will also facilitate the circle's rapid merging into a combined power-flow channel.

The basic elements of circle sharing are:

A. Gathering the energy and setting up a flow. This is done by calling forth the Light from within each heart, sharing the Light heart to heart and hand to hand.

B. Inviting and invoking the presence of Higher Powers. This can be a simple "God be with us" prayer, or a naming of Be-ings and categories of Be-ings. Examples will be given.

C. A statement of intention, well-defined, as to how/where/-with whom the Light is to be shared.

D. The conscious intentional sending of the Light to the chosen focal point or points.

EXAMPLE 1

This is a simple one-size-fits-all non-denominational circle meditation, suitable for any group. Begin by standing in a circle, joined hand to hand. The leader guides the circle along the following lines:

Take a deep breath ... relax ... breathe deeply ... relax ... Let the cares of the day fall away from you. Relax. Set them aside. Let the concerns in your life be set aside. Let them go. Relax. Breathe in the breath of Life, the breath of God. With every inhaled breath, the breath of Life, the breath of God. With every out-breath, exhale the old, tired, stale spent energies ... the frustration and pain ... the anger and fear ...let them go.

Call forth the Light from your own heart and let it fill you completely. Your own true Light, the God-Self (Goddess-Self) within you, see how it shines ... see how it feels ...

Let the energy flow from hand to hand in the circle. You receive energy from the person on your left and give energy to the person on your right. Feel the flow, around the circle. Let it flow ...

Now send forth a beam of Light, your own true inner Light, from the heart chakra directly to the heart chakra of every other person in the circle ... you interconnect with LightLines, heart to heart ... feel the energy glow ... envision the web of Light within the circle, heart to heart ...

Now take another deep breath and invoke the presence of guides and masters, angels and arch-angels, Be-ings of Light, teachers and beloved ones ... call them by name, if you wish. Only those who are recognized as "Higher Powers" or Spirit representatives and helpers should be invoked. If you wish to include loved ones who have crossed over, they should be invited rather than invoked.

Feel the Light! ... feel the Presence! ... feel the Energy! ... feel the Power! ... we are One!

Let the Light flow forth from this circle of Love ... see it grow! Send it past this room ... filling this building (or this space) .. send it all over this neighborhood ... fill the whole city with it! Send it out ... Lightlines ... we are a beacon of Light ...

And so it is.

EXAMPLE 2

This one is a quick invocation, which can be used with or without the ceremonial circle-of-sharing pattern:

May God be with us now, and at all times.
May God be with us here, and everywhere.

May God guard and guide us in this, and in all things.
And so it is.

These are examples we share with you, from our own usage. You can make up your own. The words aren't magic; there isn't any formula you have to follow. It's the *intention* that makes the magic.

EXAMPLE 3

This one is given in Native American style, without being a true representation of any one tribal tradition. Here again, you can draw from the example to stimulate ideas of your own which are in keeping with the theme and style. Anyone may walk the Red Path. A good heart is more important than mere knowledge.

O Great Spirit, hear us now.
O Great Spirit, hear us now.
O Great Spirit, hear us now.

To the North ... (offer tobacco and raise arms aloft in greeting)
To the South ... (offer tobacco and raise arms aloft in greeting)

To the East ... (offer tobacco and raise arms aloft in greeting)
To the West ... (offer tobacco and raise arms aloft in greeting)

Mother Earth, we gather in your presence. Ho!
Your sacred ground we walk upon, with every step we take.
Father Sky, we gather in your presence. Ho!
Your sacred Spirit we share, with every breath we take.

All are welcome, we invite you.
All are welcome, we invite you.
All are welcome, we invite you.
All our relations, all our relations, all our relations.
Those that creep and crawl and swim, and those who go upon four legs and two.
The winged ones.
All our relations, all our relations, all our relations.

Great Spirit, hear us now.
Great Spirit, be with us.
Great Spirit, honor us with your presence.
We are One.

You can build an infinite variety of opening (or closing) circles of sharing, along this theme. Among the presences often invoked in various Native American traditions are Spirits representing the elements (Northwind, Southwind, Eastwind, Westwind, Grandfather Fire, Mother of Waters, Great Mother of the Sea, etc.) and other aspects of nature such as Grandmother Sage, Sister Willow, Brother (or Sister) Crystals, and so forth. Every title should designate a family relationship.

The trees and rocks and streams are our relations; all creatures great and small. All Be-ings. All life. Everything is Life. When you honor them by naming them, in the Native American way, you are recognizing your kinship with them as creations, as Be-ings of the Universe. Spirit is in all. Spirit is in *all.*

EXAMPLE 4: THE MANY FACES OF THE GODDESS

Goddess rituals are among the richest, most varied and most expressive ceremonies being practiced today. There is a wealth of detailed material available in literature on the traditions and expressions of women's spirituality, notably *The Women's Spirituality Book, All Women Are Healers, and Casting the Circle*, all by Diane Stein. Another excellent feminist resource is *Woman Worship, Woman Song*, by Sister Therese Winter.

Joseph Campbell's definitive works on the history, ethno-social and psychospiritual implications of myth are also rich in Goddess lore. These are simply a few of the sources too numerous to mention.

You are already more familiar with Goddess ceremonies than you may know. Saying the rosary or lighting a candle at Mary's station, for example, are Goddess rituals as expressed within the context of the Roman Catholic faith.

This Native American chant and circle dance is a Goddess ritual:

The Earth is our Mother, we must take care of her...
The Earth is our Mother, we must take care of her...
The Earth is our Mother, we must take care of her...
Her sacred ground we walk upon, with every step
we take ...
Her sacred ground we walk upon, with every step
we take ...
Her sacred ground we walk upon, with every step
we take.

Ceremonies - expressions of energy - centered upon recognition and affirmation of Goddess power is an imaging of Universal I-Am LifeForce presence in feminine gender aspect.

Goddess ceremonies are demonstrations of respect for the principle of woman as an empowered and empowering co-creator Being. Like other ceremonies, they are tools for spiritual exploration and growth. They can be a powerful force in supporting personal emergence and the development of women who feel unempowered in a male-dominant society, and toward restoring a balanced awareness of self-worth in those who have been abused or discriminated against on the basis of gender.

Because the Earthplanet itself is generally referred to as a feminine principle, Mother Earth, Goddess ceremonies are also a path toward closer communion with the planet itself. This is equally true for persons of both genders. The EarthMother loves *all* her children.

Here is our version of a very short Goddess ceremony, meant to be sung and danced:

MotherLight, MotherLight, shining on me ...
MotherLight, MotherLight, all blessings be.

If you want it longer, you can extemporize:

Miriam, Isis, and Mary, Kwan Yin,
Bless me and bless me, and bless me again.
Maya, Inanna, and EarthMother All,
Hold me in Love and hear me when I call.
MotherLight, MotherLight, shining on me ...
Woman in you, be the Woman in me.

The point of this ceremony is that it's easy. It lends itself to personalization and participation. Use your creative imagination! Develop your own Goddess ceremony.

EXAMPLE 5: COLOR AND TONING LIGHTWAVE MEDITATIONS

This is a powerful self-healing and earth-healing exercise. It has the effect of stimulating direct energy flow, including direct energy release from the spontaneous giving up of attachments or blockages. It is best practiced within a crystal circle or grid - so that any negative energies released by individual participants will be cleared by the circle and not transferred from one person to another or otherwise allowed to remain in the area.

This is also a *loud* exercise - so you will need to practice it when and where it is not likely to over-excite your neighbors!

This exercise begins with an opening circle similar to that described in the first exercise, above, in which the Light is called forth from within and connected hand to hand and heart to heart. The presence and participation of Higher Powers are invoked.

Each member of the circle is directed to ground herself and himself, by connecting to the earth. Visualize the growing of roots, and the connective energy flow through your bodies and the circle, between Mother Earth and Father Sky.

You may either continue to hold hands or let go each others' hands, for the toning. The leader (or a pair of leaders, or a threesome) may also stand in the center of the circle if you wish. Those in the center of the circle will stand with their backs to each other, facing the outer circle. At some point, you may also wish to have everyone facing outward in the circle, rather than inward toward each other. Use your instincts! Be creative!

And as you do so, notice how the vibrational flow changes from one position and one color/tone segment to the next.

When the toning begins, everyone is invited to join in. Each one sounds the tones he and she feels moved to bring forth, and moves freely from one to another. This differs from the "Om" chanting in that there is no single given note to be sounded; everyone follows their own inner guidance.

Although the toning sometimes has moments of harmonious beauty, there should be no striving for harmony or even for that which is pleasing to the ear. The goal is vibrational, rather than musical, and some of the most vibrationally effective tones and tonal combinations are quite disharmonious and unmusical to the ear.

The sequence given below can be visualized and toned in its entirety or in any part. You need not complete the full color sequence to receive benefit. You may choose any section to work with at any given time, and these color-and-tone exercises can be done alone as well as with a group.

The leader announces which color range is to be visualized, and guides the flow from one color section to another. It is well to pause between color sections and feel the vibration, as indicated.

Here is a sample of what the leader's part might consist of (after the circle of sharing has been opened, and you are ready to begin the color and tone process):

We will begin with earthtones, rich and brown, rust and russet, with flecks of cream and orange, moving into a rich vibrant crimson red ... all the colors of red; all the variations there are, from deepest almost-black blood red to delicate pale pink. Ready ... begin with earthtone browns, and flow into reds and pinks ... red, the color of life. Bright red LifeForce.

(The leader sounds a note - any note - and each participant joins in, without seeking unison or harmony. The sounds and color flow together, creating vibrational shifts in the bodies of each person and in the group's auric field.)

> *Pause ...stop for a moment and sense your body ... feel the vibration ... take a deep breath ... remember, you are the connecting link between Father Sky and Mother Earth ... let the energy flow, in your body ...*
>
> *Now the full range of orange colors, vibrant and rich, shining with crystal flecks of light ... brilliant orange, color of sexual expression and creativity ...*

Follow the same procedure and pattern with each color range, in rainbow and chakra order, pausing between each color or between every two colors to sense vibration, stretch and breathe deeply. The naming of the chakra functions associated with each color is optional.

When you come into the green range, you may wish to take advantage of the healing aspect and bathe the group entirely in swirls of green Light ... all the greens, name the different greens as they flow from chartreuse through Kelly green to forest green and into the blue-green aquamarine range.

In the blue color group, you would flow from aquamarine and turquoise through pale blue to rich vibrant "true blue". Before moving on into indigo, you will want to add a subsection of *steel* blues and with them note the toning will have a metallic edge to it. This often produces an extremely powerful vibration to which some persons are overly sensitive. It is well to mention this beforehand, and let people know that if the vibrations are too powerful for their comfort they may leave the circle and stand aside, or even leave the room, without giving offense.

It is helpful not to stop for a sensing break between blue and indigo - move from blue into the steel blues and from there directly into indigo, then either go directly into the violet range or pause for a conscious sensing of the vibrations.

As you move through the violet colors toward white, it often happens that the toning moves spontaneously toward harmony. If not, the leader can say, *"We are now moving toward harmony, our toning is becoming beautiful, we are sharing a making of music, with each other and with the Universe."*

After a pause for sensing of the vibrational effects of the violet and white toning segments, you may wish to briefly mention some of the ways in which color is known to have an impact on behavior, and music has traditionally been used to shift vibrational frequencies and move energies. There are the mantras and the hymns, the chants and the songs.

This gives you an opportunity to lead the group in a grand *"Om"*, in unison, or to share a familiar mantra, chant or hymn in which everyone joins in. These are powerful bonding rituals, when consciously practiced as such. An easy song or chant also smooths the transition from a perception of being involved in extra-normal or super-normal activity to the familiar mundane "normal" focus again, and is therefore an excellent way to wrap up a session of group ceremonial exercises.

If you choose to sing something with words, make sure the words are inclusive (i.e., non-exclusive with regard to gender, race, and so forth), non-conflictive (not warlike), and stated in an empowered, power-within base, not in a power-over language base. You'll be amazed at how many well beloved Christian hymns don't meet those standards!

"Trust and obey, for there's no other way" ... "Amazing grace, how sweet the sound that saved a wretch like me ..." Are those empowering concepts? We certainly wouldn't class them as *negatives;* their intent is strongly positive. A good heart means more than technical details. However, they aren't entirely suitable for a power-within based group energy exercise.

Ceremonies are expressions of energy. To assure that your ceremonies will be empowered and empowering, that they will be positive tools for transformation, consider the energies - including the language base - of which they are composed.

For examples of power-within based language, look to the hymnals of Unity or other churches which specifically affirm the power-within principle in their teachings. The hymnals of many denominations have also been recently revised to reflect inclusive and empowering language - use your instincts and good judgment.

Here are some obvious "winners":

"Om Nava Shivaya"
"Let There Be Peace on Earth"
"The Earth Is Our Mother"
"Alleluia, Alleluia" (many versions!)
"Dona Nobis Pacem"

Of course, you can also create your own songs. Here are some examples from our channel's unpublished files:

This one is for a closing circle. It is set to a simple tune anyone can learn.

CIRCLES OF LIGHT

Circles of Light joined hand to hand,
Gathering now, our little band.
Circles of Love joined heart to heart;
We meet in Light; in Light and Love
so shall we part.
Sharing the joy; sharing the tears,
Shedding our cares; calming our fears.
We are all One, bonded in Love,
Those here below joined in the Light
by those above.

Sing Mother Earth,
Sing Father Sky.
Rainbows abound,
Filling our eyes.
Sing for the Self,
And for the All;
Sing for the touch ...
of Spirit's call.

Circles of Light joined hand to hand,

Saying goodbye, our little band.
Circles of Love joined heart to heart;
We met in Light, in Light and Love
now let us part.

This one has a Native American flavor and musical style. It is more appropriate to a personal ceremony (expression of energy) than for a group exercise.

FLY AWAY
(dedicated to the Winged Ones)

Tell me a tale of a new breeze blowing;
Sing me a song of spirit in the land *
and I'll fly away ...
fly away.

I'll fly away on the wings of an eagle,
soaring golden in the sun;
see with his eyes as I fly with the eagle,
we are One.

Sing me the joy of new heart's-knowing;
Sing me a song of spirit in the land
and I'll fly away ...
fly away.

I'll fly away on the wings of a hawk,
Above the river and the trees;
Fly on the wings of a hawk, I'm in her
and she's in me.

Whisper a sigh of a new moon glowing;
Sing me a song of spirit in the land
and I'll fly away ...
fly away.

I'll fly away on the wings of an owl,
He is the eagle of the night;
Sail through the dark with the owl
and receive the gift of sight.

Sing me the joy of a new self-knowing;
Sing me a song of spirit in the land
and I'll fly away ...
fly away ...
fly away ...
fly away ...

*Optional: Instead of "*Sing me a song of spirit in the land,*" substitute "*Chant me a mantra of spirit in the land,*" wherever this line appears.

You can create your own ceremonies. You can make your own music. You can enrich your life and the lives of others around you in so many ways. You can heal yourself, and support the self-healing of others and of the planet. You are unlimited Be-ings.

Think about how the music of your life has created vibrational shifts, and moved energy. Think of how it has brought you closer to one another and to the figures of your faith - or has distanced you from them, if it is filled with power-over concept language base and/or a vehicle for negative energy.

Think of how rock bands use light shows with their music, to intensify the experience of their audiences. Think of how music videos use color, form and sound to create effects which touch people's response centers and alter their personal vibrations.

Color and sound visualizations/tonings are powerful tools for supporting the healing of the self, others and the planet. They are powerful tools for expanding one's inner vision, clearing blockages, and connecting with the Universe.

Chapter 12

The Use of Crystals and Stones In Support of Healing and Personal Development

Crystal energies are highly interactive with human energies. The piesoelectric qualities of the crystal can be directly integrated with the electrochemical properties of the brain, through intention or through pre-existing affinity.

In Native American and other early earth-planet traditions, they are often culturally associated with Father Sky, i.e., with the mystical, magical or godlike qualities of that which lies beyond ordinary mortal ken. This association is reflected in Judeo-Christian Biblical text - Aaron's breastplate - and in Egyptian, Celtic, Norse, Oriental, Hindu and other mythic traditions. You can recognize references to crystals and their power in stories of Merlin's wand, the Grail, jeweled third eye and navel adornments of Buddhist and Hindu figures, and so forth.

Stone energies also interact with human vibrational frequency. They are traditionally associated with Mother Earth, and often provide a calming, "grounding", balancing influence.

In general, crystals tend to be clear and stones tend to be opaque. Within a given class of crystal or stone, however, there is a wide variation in individual clarity or opacity.

Clear crystals (or sections of crystal) are often called "male" and those that are milky are often called "female". This is an accurate reflection of their base of primary association with Mother Earth and/or Father Sky. As individual humans often exhibit traits associated with traditional ways of expressing male embodiment *and* traits associated with traditional ways of expressing female embodiment, so individual crystals also exhibit mixed male and female characteristics.

The use of crystals and stones in supporting self-healing has unlimited potential. The listing below represents only the tip of the iceberg!

The **AGATES** lend themselves to a wide variety of general and specific uses. In general, agate tends to be calm, grounding and balancing. In specific, particular types of agate often embody the memory-energy of other planets and their characteristics as related to the earthplanet.

Picture agate can often stimulate past-life memory as it relates to a particular series of non-terrestrial planetary incarnations.

Blue lace agate is useful in connecting with one's angelic guardians, especially the so-called "Solar" angels of Ra Energies Complex origin.

AMETHYST is a quartz variety that varies in color from pale lavender-pink to deep violet. It is a "user-friendly" stone: highly versatile, and easy for beginners to access. It is widely used for protection, purification, channeling, healing, inspiration, and metaphysical awakening. Like clear quartz, it can be pressed into service for almost any purpose. It is most commonly used with crown or third eye chakras.

Clear amethysts that are deeply colored are especially useful in connecting with the Higher Self and Universal Light energies. The deeper colorations are also prized for their metaphysical or "magical" power, and often used in wands, grids, jewelry, and other personal adornment or working tool capacities. Pale lavender and pink amethysts are especially useful in generating gentle pain-control energies in instances where a more overtly powerful energy might be overstimulating.

Guadelajara amethysts are natural sucking-stones; they draw out the poisons from the body. Amethyst phantoms are particularly useful in promoting the healing of the inner child and development of the inner self.

AQUA-AURA crystals are clear quartz that have been infused with gold at the molecular bonding level. They are one of the few non-natural crystals we recommend for protective and healing use, and are as versatile as clear quartz. The crystal's natural vibrational frequency rate is speeded up by interaction with the gold, which is highly conductive, and there is a consequent amplification of energy impact.

AQUAMARINE is a variety of beryl which may be used to open the throat chakra and stimulate clarity of self-communication as well as communication with others. It also assists in promoting creativity, calm, confidence and balance. It is sometimes also used at the power chakra, as a stimulus to promote *peaceful* use of personal power.

Green **AVENTURINE** promotes emotional balance and tranquility and aids in releasing fears or anxieties through purification of the mental, emotional and etheric bodies. It assists in balancing the blood and muscle tissues. Some people use it in centering, or associate it with prosperity, independence, and well-being. On layouts for healing, it is usually used with the heart chakra.

AZURITE's copper content enhances energy flow throughout the nervous system. It stimulates the throat chakra and promotes clarity of self-communication through absorption of stagnant energies in the etheric body. At the third eye chakra, it stimulates intuition and creativity.

Natural rough (unpolished) azurite functions as a "sucking" crystal directly at the etheric body level, absorbing misaligned energies. After use, the azurite should be cleansed by any of the usual methods, such as washing in cool water, blowing briskly across it (the "Breath of Life" cleansing), placing it in a magnetic field for half an hour, setting it on the window sill to absorb sun and moon rays for a few days, and so forth.

BLOODSTONE is aptly named. This chalcedony variety strengthens and oxygenates the bloodstream, heart, spleen, bone marrow and promotes physical and mental vitality. It relates to both heart and root chakras, and is a strong physical healer - especially for those who are said to be "broken-hearted" or "have lost the will to live".

CALCITE is grounding, and removes excess energy. It is an excellent "worry stone" for the nervous or overexcitable, and tends to reduce stress. It can be used in combination with other stones for chakra work, and also helps to balance male/female polarities.

In some (but not all) persons, calcite aids in astral projection.

In healing, it is most often used to work with kidneys, pancreas and spleen.

CARNELIAN is a vital, energizing variety of chalcedony. Depending on the color, clarity and character of the individual piece, it can be used as a powerful stimulus toward clearing blocked second or third chakras. Toward healing of specific organs, carnelian is often used to support the self-healing of blood (as an energizer), kidneys, lungs, liver, gallbladder, pancreas, and tissue regeneration.

CELESTITE promotes healthy thyroid function, reduces stress, enhances relaxation and peace of mind. Stimulates accelerated awakening and supports freedom of self-expression. It is used at the throat chakra, and especially stimulates intuitive communication.

CHRYSOCOLLA is considered by many to be a preventative against ulcers, digestive problems, and arthritic conditions. Its use is also associated with strengthening of thyroid and lungs, metabolism, and female reproductive organs.

In the emotional body, chrysocolla reduces fear, guilt and tension, and helps in clearing subconscious blockages. It also stimulates creativity and joyfulness, and is used primarily with the throat and heart chakras.

CITRINE is a variety of quartz that is especially useful in chakra balancing or opening blocked chakras. Dark orange colored citrine is used with the second chakra, lighter colored pieces are used with the third chakra. Citrine is also considered beneficial toward healing of kidneys, colon, liver, gallbladder, digestive organs and heart.

It promotes tissue regeneration, assists in detoxifying physical, emotional and mental bodies, and supports the body's self-healing energies by diminishing self-destructive tendencies, raising self-esteem and stimulating alignment with the higher self. Used at the crown chakra, it is said to draw the vigorous productivity that creates abundance.

DIAMONDS are highly complex in function. They tend to amplify the energy expression *and intention* of the user, and to hold their programming indefinitely. Used for healing, they enhance brain function, break up blockages in crown chakra and in the personality. They are capable of serving as master healers to dispel negativity, purify and heal physical and etheric bodies. They can be used with all chakras.

Diamonds reflect the will and power aspects of self and God-self; they amplify and enhance the full spectrum of energies in body, mind and spirit. They are extremely open to the intent of the user, and among those who seek enLightment a diamond promotes alignment with the higher self, abundance, innocence, purity and faithfulness.

In earthplanet history, there have also been instances of diamonds being used to transmit or hold negative energies. The stone is a faithful servant of the user - not an expression of its own inherent qualities - and can therefore be "cursed", i.e., programmed in negative alignment. Therefore, diamonds should be cleansed/cleared and reprogrammed for positive function as they change hands and are acquired by new owners.

DIOPTASE supports the cardiovascular and central nervous systems, and is used to combat ulcers, nervous stomach, heart trouble, and blood pressure imbalances. It is another of the user-friendly stones that can easily be used by those who are just getting acquainted with crystal usage. There is little or no danger of over-stimulation or counter-productive use of dioptase, and at the same time it can be quite strong as a healing tool.

It vitalizes/balances body and mind, promotes peace of mind, and supports emotional stability. Is widely used as an enhancement with affirmations for health, abundance, prosperity, progress, and general well-being. It is most widely used with the heart chakra and the secondary chakras at the arch of each foot.

EMERALD is a variety of beryl. In ordinary usage, it strengthens heart, liver, kidneys, immune system and the nervous system, acting as a tonic for body, mind and spirit. Emeralds also enhance dreams, meditation and spiritual insight and are associated with prosperity, love, kindness, tranquility, balance, healing, patience, and emotional balance. They are most widely used with heart and power chakras.

In its history of extraordinary usage on this planet, emerald is keyed closely to persons with clear green or blue-green eyes, and has the potential power to awaken their natural metaphysical gifts, enabling them to see through the stone even when the stone is at a distance.

Worn at the third eye or around the neck, a clear (and highly polished) gem-quality emerald promotes the opening of the so-called second sight and is said to assist in providing psychic sight to those whose physical sight is lacking or impaired. Jewel emeralds have been highly prized for use in crowns, tiaras and necklaces (often amplified by being set with diamonds) throughout the ages.

FLUORITE is said to be good for teeth and bones; it promotes the absorption of vital nutrients. It's also good for spleen and blood vessels, especially in strengthening delicate veins. The predominately green pieces (especially those dug in China) can be quite calming, balancing, grounding. The lavender and violet pieces tend to stimulate psychic experience, including out-of-body travel, and can be overstimulating to those who are susceptible.

Fluorite can lift you out of yourself. Someone who has difficulty in concentrating or meditating might use a purple fluorite to assist in setting the mundane focus aside and grasping higher and more abstract concepts. The stone also facilitates interdimensional communication and can be a powerful healer. It can be used with various chakras and attitudes according to color of stone.

The **RED GARNET** strengthens, purifies, vitalizes and regenerates all body systems. It is good for the bloodstream through strong interaction with the root chakra, and is also used to open, support and balance root chakra energies.

In healing, the red or green garnet can be used equally well with the heart chakra. These two stones are particularly helpful when used in conjunction with each other, to combat irregular heart rhythm.

GREEN GARNETS can be placed along the spine from the base of the skull to the base of the spine to align energy flow in the spine and connective tissues. An odd number of garnets should preferably be used - five, seven or nine - rather than an even number. They are particularly helpful for slipped or ruptured disc and pinched nerve injuries.

JADE offers strong protective and healing vibrations. It is another of the stones we consider to be particularly suitable for the novice. It fends off negative energies and stimulates positive ones.

Jade strengthens heart, kidneys, immune system, and blood. It promotes longevity and fertility, and is particularly helpful with eye disorders and female problems.

In the emotional body, its influence is both calming and strengthening. It is a balancing stone that radiates confidence and love. It is historically associated with clarity, modesty, courage, justice, wisdom, peacefulness and nurturing. It is the stone most closely associated with the Buddha and with Kwan Yin, the Goddess of Mercy.

Jade's healing properties can be used with any chakra, regardless of the color of the stone.

KUNZITE is the most powerful heart-opener of all the crystals. It relates specifically to the etheric heart, which is the eighth major chakra now in the process of awakening in humankind. Like the new chakra, Kunzite relates to unconditional love and cosmic communication. Its high lithium content also makes it beneficial to those choosing to overcome addictive behavior. It strengthens the cardiovascular system and is said to aid manic depression.

Kunzite balances physical, emotional, mental and spiritual bodies and enhances self-esteem. It is used primarily with the heart and (new) thymus chakras.

LAPIS LAZULI is an excellent protective stone for animals and for those whose vibrational frequency is modest, static or blocked. Once programmed for protection, it holds a steady flow of protective energy with little or no need for conscious reinforcement. It also strengthens the skeletal system, activates the thyroid gland, releases tension and anxiety and energizes the throat chakra. It tends to augment strength, vitality, and virility.

Lapis Lazuli - especially when used in tandem with kunzite - can facilitate the opening of any chakra. It is associated with mental clarity, illumination, creativity, psychic abilities and communication with one's higher self and spirit guides.

It is especially useful in clearing blockages of the minor chakras at the instep of the foot and palm of the hand, and (in those who are entering into exploration and use of the more esoteric supplemental chakras) can be used at the base of the skull and nape of the neck to activate the subtler functions of the limbic system.

LEPIDOLITE interacts with muscles, heart, and blood to promote overall healing of the physical body. Its high lithium content helps in emotional/mental balance and stability, aids sleep, and supports expression of one's inner light and joy.

In the etheric body, lepidolite assists in integrating levels of consciousness and levels of energy. In that context it is used in conjunction with the crown and eighth (thymus) chakras. It can also be used simultaneously placed at heart and sexual chakras, to connect the two (in instances where emotion - love - and sexual function have become disconnected or distanced from each other).

MALACHITE is a real workhorse, among healing stones. It

aids the function of pancreas and spleen, tissue regeneration, brain, heart, circulatory system, pineal and pituitary glands. It reduces stress and tension, acts as a balancer on all levels, and supports restful sleep.

Malachite is most commonly used with heart and solar plexus chakras. It can also be used effectively at the joints (elbows, wrists, knees, ankles, etc.), to break up blockages, and at the sinus nodes to drain sinus headaches.

Although intentional empowerment can be used to boost its effectiveness, malachite doesn't require conscious programming to function and can easily be beneficial to people who are distracted or unawakened.

MARBLE has an extensive history of interaction with human energy. As a building stone it tends to be grounding and calming. Used in public buildings and halls of government, for example, it tends to absorb the excess and undirected energy which is often characteristic of humans who legislate, adjudicate, teach or conduct business there. At the subconscious and energy-interaction levels, the marble floors, columns, stairs and walls themselves whisper subtly of respectful infinity. They absorb excess noise (it is not the marble itself that produces an echo-chamber effect, but rather the spaciousness that is associated with marble halls) and balance scattered personal energies.

Marble is also used for statues, decorations and decorative implements (such as bookends, fountains, etc.) and personal stones. Here again, the overall effect is to bring calm, balance, a sense of peace and well-being. Overexcitement and stress are lessened. Marble promotes personal and group stability.

MOLDAVITE is a deep green silica-based tektite (meteorite) which promotes extraterrestrial contact (whether internal or external) and aids in alignment with the higher self. There is no better stone for aiding channeling of extraterrestrial and interdimensional sources. It is usually used with the heart and third eye chakras.

Moldavite is also a powerful "shamanstone", exhibiting powerfully protective vibrations and enabling the user to overcome a wide range of obstacles.

MOONSTONE is associated with love, stability and female empowerment. It has a healing affinity for stomach, spleen, pancreas, and pituitary gland and tends to overcome blocks in the lymphatic system. An emotional balancer, it relieves stress and anxiety and helps lessen tendency to overreact emotionally through promoting calm and confidence.

Moonstone aids birthing process, and is used to clear and balance female sexual or reproductive concerns. It also promotes flexibility in attitude and aligns emotions with the Higher self. It is most commonly used with the heart, etheric heart and sexual chakras.

OBSIDIAN carries a slightly masculine energy, and tends to call forth blocked emotional and/or past life energies from the subconscious, allowing them to be released from the body. Held in the palm or placed under the pillow, it can be used to stimulate the release of energies in dreamtime. Pure black obsidian (Apache tears) is best used for that purpose.

Snowflake obsidian is especially helpful for stomach and intestines. It is an excellent "worry stone", that calms unreasonable fears and reduces stress.

Obsidian is usually used with the root chakra. It can also be used with the crown chakra to calm the idle chatter of the brain and open doorways to the Universe beyond the smaller focus of self.

PERIDOT protects against negative energy (including psychic attack), draws prosperity (especially when used with affirmations for self-appreciation and abundance), increases intuitive awareness, and accelerates personal growth. It is also a powerful tool for self-healing support.

Peridot balances the glandular system, aids in tissue regeneration, purifies the body (especially the circulatory system), and has a beneficial influence on heart, pancreas, spleen, liver, and adrenals. It reduces stress and overcomes stress-induced blockages in the subconscious.

In more esoteric usage, it assists in balancing/aligning the various levels of auric and etheric energies. In the mental body, it builds confidence and opens new doors of opportunity. It is used with the navel, solar plexus, heart, and crown chakras.

CLEAR QUARTZ is extremely versatile, and can be used to support almost any healing or developmental purpose. It is used with all chakras (including those of the etheric bodies, beyond the physical) and enhances the crystalline properties of blood, body and mind.

It activates and enhances pineal and pituitary glands, and

serves as an emotional balancer. It stimulates brain functions by direct interaction of its piesoelectric properties with the electro-chemical process of the brain, and amplifies thought forms. Its full spectrum energy activates all levels of consciousness.

It dispels negativity in one's energy field and in one's environment. Clear quartz crystals that are used as adornment and decoration tend to purify the persons who wear them and the spaces in which they are placed. Their ability to receive, activate, store, transmit, focus and amplify energy has led to their widespread industrial use. They are excellent for meditation, and tend to enhance interdimensional communication and alignment with higher self and spirit guides.

In healing layouts or grids, clear quartz can be used as a substitute for other stones which may not be readily available. If you want the quartz to mimic and emit the energies characteristics to another stone, simply hold the quartz crystal in your hand and visualize the stone that is needed. You might express your intention clearly by saying, "Be a peridot!" or "You are now a rhodochrosite." Remember to de-program the clear quartz when you are finished.

Clear quartz crystals are extremely versatile and can be used for any positive purpose. While it is true that the intentional use of quartz (and other crystals) for negative purpose does have some historical validity, that is no longer feasible. The crystals themselves, as a class, have aligned with Light-energy and will not permit themselves to be wrongly used.

They do need to be cleaned and purified, however, to remove accumulations of a scum-like energy which dulls their surface and impairs their fuller function.

RHODOCHROSITE emits vibrations of Divine love, self-acceptance, tolerance of others, and serves as a powerful healer of emotional wounds and traumas. It aids the spleen, kidneys, heart, pituitary gland and circulation of the blood.

In the mental body, it enhances memory and intellectual power. It supports courage, an impassioned zest for life and sharing, and right use of will, and is an emotional balancer.

In the subtle bodies, rhodochrosite assists in balancing through blending the vibrations of root, crown, heart and power chakras.

RUTILATED QUARTZ enhances the expression of LifeForce,

strengthens the immune system, and aids in regeneration of tissue throughout body. It stimulates brain functions, eases depression, facilitates inspiration, and enhances clairvoyance.

Its piesoelectric properties are stronger than those of clear quartz, so its impact on the user is intensified. It transmutes negativity and enhances communication with one's Higher self and spirit guides. It can be used with all the chakras, and is a powerful healer.

SAPPHIRE promotes self-expression and clarity of communication with the self and others. It stimulates psychic abilities, inspiration, creativity, loyalty, and love.

Sapphire expands cosmic awareness and dispels confusion. It is excellent for meditation. It also strengthens heart and kidneys, and activates pituitary gland, thereby aiding entire glandular system. It is used with throat, third eye and etheric heart chakras and assists in balancing of body/mind/spirit.

SMOKY QUARTZ has a history of being used as a power crystal and is an excellent choice for protective shielding or defensive weaponry. It also dissipates negativity within the self, and aids in overcoming blocks in the subconscious. It promotes self-confidence, energizes the mental and emotional bodies, and dispels depression.

Some people find smoky quartz to be mildly sedative and relaxing. It also strengthens the adrenals, kidneys, pancreas, balances sexual energy and increases fertility.

It enhances dream awareness and is an excellent crystal to take into shamanic dreamtime journey. It is excellent for meditation and supports channeling abilities. Its grounding and centering properties assist in keeping one's balance during metaphysical exploration and returning to mundane reality comfortably. It is most often used with the root, navel, or solar plexus chakras, and with the chakras at the palms of the hands.

SUGILITE has strongly protective qualities. It is used for channeling and meditation, and integrates higher spiritual awareness into the physical body. While it enhances personal sensitivity, it is balanced and also has the ability to shield against over-sensitivity. The wearing of sugilite can make one less painfully sensitive to the ills of the world, such as the woes that are regularly viewed on the evening television news program. It reduces stress.

Sugilite enhances the functions of pineal, pituitary and adrenal glands. It activates and balances the brain hemispheres. This versatile stone also strengthens the heart, and supports physical healing and purification of bodily systems. It is usually used at the third eye and crown chakras, and can also be used at heart, etheric heart and solar plexus.

TIGER EYE is a variety of chalcedony which is beneficial for the spleen, pancreas, digestive organs, and colon. A popular choice for "worry stones" or good luck pieces, it is also an emotional balancer and enhances the connection with personal power and will.

It is grounding and centering, helps soften stubbornness, and enhances clear perception and insight. It is said to have a slightly masculine energy, yet also carries a strong Goddess-energy connection as a basic earthstone. It is used at the navel and solar plexus chakras, and can also be placed at the third eye to gain insight into earth issues and earth changes.

TOURMALINE (there are several colors) is one of the most powerful of healing stones. It strengthens and vitalizes body, mind and spirit through activating and enhancing the crystalline properties of body and mind. As an aid to sleep, it also promotes lucid and healing dreaming.

Tourmaline assists in balancing the endocrine system, aligns subtle bodies, dispels fear and negativity. It has a strong protective influence, and a particular color-alignment known as "watermelon" tourmaline is called Christstone. It promotes concentration, inspiration, spirituality, sensitivity and understanding. Some cancers respond particularly well to the use of Christstone for self-healing support.

Tourmaline is highly electromagnetic, and serves as a powerful healer. The various colors will especially activate and align corresponding chakras - black tourmaline for root, watermelon for root, heart and etheric heart, green for heart, blue for throat and third eye, red or pink for root and heart, etc. - and any color can also be used in tandem with clear quartz to amplify the energies of any chakra.

TURQUOISE calms, tones, and strengthens the entire body. It supports tissue regeneration, especially in the circulatory and respiratory systems.

It aids in aligning chakras and enhances meditation, creative expression, peace of mind, emotional balance, communication, friendship, and loyalty. It is used at the throat and foot chakras, and the less common color varieties can be used at the chakras of corresponding color.

Turquoise is also helpful in promoting coolness from within the self, and protects against overheating in hot climates.

There is a great deal of information about crystals and stones which has not yet been commonly shared with you. We look forward to having an opportunity to explore the subject further with you, in the future.

Crystals, gems and other minerals are used as tools for personal transformation. You appreciate their beauty, usefulness and stimulating influence and often come to think of them as "friends". In using them to support self-healing or for any purpose, it is well to remember that the stone does not create an intention. It *supports* your intention. The power does not belong to the stone. ***The power is your own!***

Chapter 13

SHARING THE VISION

Even as you are in the process of solving today's problems and creating today's joyful good health, you are also looking ahead to bold new visions of higher levels of personal and planetary wellbeing.

The fearful specters of infirmity, decay, helpless old age, struggle against dis-ease and eventual reluctant death have already faded from your consciousness.

No-one has to die. Sometimes death is a good choice. It's an individual decision. In your lifetime, ascension is also an option. A valid choice, accessible to you.

No-one has to be dis-eased. Your bodies do not necessarily have to decay and weaken. Those are choices you can make, if you wish. Or you may choose vibrant good health, in every cell, every tissue, every organ of your body and in every fibre of your body/mind/spirit Be-ing.

No matter what your present bodily condition, vibrant good health is an option you may freely choose. It's not too late to make the choice, and take action to implement your decision.

Joy is the greatest wisdom. Joy is the greatest teacher. The greatest service is joyful and fulfilling. Let us suppose for a moment that you are willing to set aside the tools for growth and service called death and disease, struggle and suffering, and choose tools called joyful self-empowerment, joyful service and joyful sharing.

Let us suppose you have joyfully solved your problems and joyfully created vibrant good health of body, mind and spirit.

Then what?

What is your *next* co-created reality?

It isn't enough to simply reject the old reality, and work toward eradicating its undesirable features. Having a clear vision of the new reality allows you to create it.

If you can dream it, you can do it.

If you are going to do it, you have to first be able to dream it. Or you can enroll in someone else's dream, someone else's vision of the new reality. You don't always have to be the first one to think of it, to claim it as your own: followers share co-creatorship with leaders, by investing their intention and energy in joint effort.

For about 98 percent of the earth's population today, the co-creative new planetary realities are beyond their wildest dreams. Yet those same new realities are already under construction and coming swiftly into being.

It happens with the flow of steadily changing ever-growing shifts of mass consciousness. These are furthered along day by day and hour by hour in the meditations, self-healing and earth-healing exercises, focus groups and other intentions and actions (including conscious or unconscious activities in dreamtime, no-time, shamanic non-ordinary realities, spirit-plane interaction, etc.) of those in the forefront of the spiritual growth movement.

And even now in the hearts and visions of the dreamers, at the leading edge of co-creative change, there are newer, brighter visions of that which is to come.

The age of transition in which you now live is an age of swift and dramatic co-creatorship in action. It is an age of overcoming limitations, of sloughing off the patterns of the past which are no longer useful to you and your society.

Are there walls and barriers? Tear them down! Are there masses of people caught in a power-over based system of government control? Change the government! Some governments are changed by votes and elected leadership; others by revolution.

You are in the process of rejecting power-over based concepts in government and business, in your society as a whole, just as you are rejecting power-over based concepts in your personal lives.

You are living in an age of *change.*

You are the agents of change. Your collectively co-created reality becomes the new norm, the new pattern of personal and cultural Be-ing of the earth. And now that yesterday's dreams - your dreams - are coming true, it also falls to you to lead the way, again, by dreaming for tomor-

row.

You are well on your way to becoming an unlimited Be-ing. You are well on your way toward joining with other unlimited Be-ings in creating a new heaven and a new earth, even as it was foretold that this would come to pass.

We are all One. Oh Best Beloveds, what shall we create together?

An expression of LifeForce energy. A place and a time unique in the vastness of the Universe. A work of art; a culmination of all the ages and expressions of co-created planetary reality which have thus far come to pass.

A place where the lion shall lie down with the lamb and conflict shall cease; where/when wars shall be no more. A garden of Allah, filled with all things lovely and pleasurable. Is not the concept of reward for the faithful a fulfillment of their co-creative dreaming?

A city not made by hands; a community of the Spirit of which we are all integral parts. A land that is fairer than day, and by faith we have seen it afar. Nirvana with its utter Oneness and Devachan with its pure delight; Tirn'an'og and Greenfields and all the rest; all these are our past and future selves, our distant homelands across the skies and our co-creative realities in process of manifesting here on planet earth.

Are these not your dreams, as well as ours? Have we not shared these dreams together, heart to heart and age to age?

They are coming true, oh Best Beloveds. And you are a part of making it happen.

There will be no more war ... when the perception of need for war, the desire for conflict between nations and cultures has been overcome.

There will be no more hunger ... when the perception that someone always goes hungry, that there isn't enough food for everyone has been overcome.

There will be no more homeless ... when the perception that there's never enough housing has been overcome.

All the things that are lacking in those lives we call "disadvantaged" will be abundantly available, once the concept of lack itself has been overcome. The challenge is to overcome the limitation. The first step toward overcoming limitation is to reject the *perception* of limitation. Stop believing in it!

The earthplanet's physical resources, in third-dimensional consensus reality, were/are finite. Limited. The earthplanet's *new* physical resources, in fourth-dimensional consensus reality, are unlimited. And the ability of LifeForce, the Life-Source's ability to weave direct spiritual energy expressions into co-creations of wondrous Be-ing is the most unlimited of all.

Believe on this, best beloveds, and you will be healed. Believe in yourselves as co-creators of the Universe, and you will become one with God.

There will be no more dis-ease and dis-comfort when the concept of every Be-ing's absolute power to heal him-self/herself/itself has been accepted. You can overcome any limitation. You will have healed yourself and your society, your planet, when the perception that you "can't" heal yourself has been rejected.

Believe on this, best beloveds, and you will be healed. Believe in yourselves. All healing is self-healing.

On With The NEW!

The new earthplanet will be *physical.* It will be a different kind of physical.

Human Be-ings and other lifeforms on the new planet will also be *physical.* They, too, will be a new kind of physical. There will be common forms and behavioral patterns, yet these will be less rigid than those you are accustomed to in third dimensional vibrational frequency - less limiting, and more empowering.

Consensus reality guidelines will be flexible. You will be fully conscious of your co-creative abilities, and can manifest choices for change with an easy combination of intention and action.

These are some of the hallmarks of the future reality we believe will be co-created on and for this planet:

- Universally accessible telepathic communication. Any individual will be able to communicate internal-ly, without the assistance of telephones or other devices, with any other individual - and will be able to tune in interactively to any and every "channel" of collective planetary consciousness, without the use of television broadcasting or receiving machinery or other devices.

- Interspecies communication (i.e., with animals and other lifeforms) will also be universally accessible. There will be no "dumb" animals; they will all be consciously interactive Be-ings as they were intended. Each has its own agreement of roles to play and ways to serve the desires of other species, including humanity.
- Eating and food will be entirely optional. Physical bodies will not require nourishment from food sources; they will be entirely sustained by direct energy. Many people will choose to manifest "food" for the enjoyment of the senses, especially in social use. The food will be directly created from free energy; the eating of "meat" will not require the taking of animal life. The eating of plants will be a conscious communion between plant and other Be-ings, or "fruits and vegetables" can also be manifested directly from free energy.
- The new society will be a very loving one, in which personal energies are shared, one with another, and group-sharing energy circles will be the norm rather than the exception. There will be no more jealousy. Love between one Be-ing and another/others will be a non-limiting unconditional sharing of personal energy, without the setting up of boundaries and barriers inherent in exclusivity agreements. In other words, there will be no marrying or giving in marriage, in heaven. All love is holy. All unions of love are holy, within the Spirit of the One, which is All.
- Sexual union, as an expression of love bonding, will be optional. You want it? You'll have it! However, there will be no negative expressions of sexual intercourse such as rape or the using of sexual favors as bargaining chips. There will be no bargaining for sex or love. That which is exchanged will be freely given by each participant, without condition or obligation.

- Shelters, homes, temples, gathering houses, and all manner of other structures will be optional, and manifested directly from free energy, at will.
- Communication with other planets throughout the Universe will be readily available, and commonly conducted. Travel between this system and other sectors of the Universe will be easy and accessible.
- Angelic Be-ings and other extraterrestrials will be commonplace as co-equal, co-creative members of earthplane society.
- The terms "living" and "dead" will be obsolete and have no practical meaning. One can become embodied (in the form of choice) or disembodied (pure energy unit) at will. There will be those who take the form of (as viewed from earthplane perspective) stars, and dance together joyfully in the night sky ... others will be butterflies upon the wind, or the wind itself slipping in and out of the willow. You will know what it is to be fire, to be water, to be crystal, all that which you choose to know will be yours.

And you will still be *you*. There is no loss of selfhood, only the gaining of many other selves to know and cherish. Each has its own richness and piquancy to be explored, to be shared.

Who knows what new wonders you will create and co-create? Only *you* know, as a beginning, in that part of you which knows all things and has not yet found full conscious expression. Every soul is that of a poet and every hand is that of an artist.

Every idea is an adventure, and every craft an invention.

Look to the past, and see how co-creative mind and hand and eye have shaped the present. Upon the third dimensional earthplanet itself, whose role in Universal cosmic and planetary interrelationship is very much that of an experimental laboratory, your co-creative imagination and resourcefulness have brought diverse objects and abundantly varied happenings into Be-ing.

Look to the present, and see how awakening mind and hand and eye are creating new realities, new diversities, upon that selfsame planet.

Look to the future, and know how unlimited co-creative

mind and hand and eye shall paint an equally rich artistic expression of multifaceted experience. You will shape this planet anew, as surely as you are now in the process of shaping your own lives and bodies anew.

Let yourself go! Make it happen!

We Are All ONE

As you walk self-chosen individual paths of Be-ing, know that you are not alone. We are all One.

As you learn lessons of life, by experience, know that your learning of lessons assists others in their growth paths. We are all One.

As your resourceful problem-solving ability envisions and identifies bold new solutions and exciting new creations, know that you are co-creating a fuller, more richly detailed and brighter reality for all of us - for the whole Universe, across its unlimited vastness. We are all One.

As you raise your eyes and thoughts from mundane here-and-now to the infinity of cosmos which lies beyond the veil of mortal ken, know that through fully manifested cosmic consciousness you will have much to gain ... and much to give. We are all One.

As you heal yourselves and your planet, know that "healing" is an energy expression which flows to and fro between this earth time/space/place and every other time/space/place. We are many, and we are all One.

As you reach for the stars, oh Best Beloveds, know that the stars are also reaching for you. We are all One.

APPENDIX 1

Footnotes

1. The Crystal Circle offers an accelerated method of healing in this context, through its channels.
2. For an excellent resource on this process as it relates to modern experience, see the book *Spiritual Emergency*. Other suggested reading on shamanism: many works of Joseph Campbell. Also: *Shamanism* by Harold Nicholson, and *Shamanism* by Mircea Eliade.
3. Magnetic healing isn't new. It's been done in the Orient for thousands of years, and in Western medicine for decades. If you research the topic in a medical library, you'll find a wide selection of material available. Some excellent books are also out on the subject, including *Magneto Therapy* by Dr. H. L. Bansal, *The Body Magnetic* by Buryl Payne and *Cross Currents* by Robert O. Becker.
4. In using terms such as "negative energies" and "psychic attack", let us clearly note that we affirm the positive nature of the Universe and the Oneness of that positivity. At Universal Oneness level there is no "negative", or "evil", or "attack"; there is only Oneness. At the earthplane experiential level in which context our comments on self-healing are given, there ***are***, regretfully, certain counter-balances of energies which may be appropriately described as "negative" or "attacking".
5. The specific techniques, procedures, tools and philosophies contained in this document are those which have been identified as the best of their genre and widely beneficial on a broad basis, in the opinion of Edgar Cayce and The Crystal Circle. We do not "prescribe" or "claim cures". We share our opinion and insight with you, for your consideration. Any action you may take (or not take) is done upon your own responsibility, and should always be carefully evaluated in the Light of your own inner guidance. The

only source of authority for you is you.

6. For further information on Magnetic Healing, consult your local medical library or bookstore. For further information on Nikken magnetic products and opportunities, please contact Laurel Steinhice, or David Sohn, P.O. Box 50145, Nashville, TN 37505 or call (615) 356-4280.
7. Natural magnets and natural magnetic field, as opposed to electromagnets and the 60-cycle electromagnetic vibration.
8. Early humanity's endorsement of the concept of "power-over" was essential to the development of the species and the planet. That principle has served well throughout guided-developmental stages of the Earthplanet growth process and it is only *now*, in the present age of transition to a new maturity, that it is being replaced by a recognition of personal co-creator responsibility called "power- within".
9. These suggestions for wellness techniques are not intended as a "cure-all" to be substituted for either traditional or nontraditional healthcare. Further information on wholistic healing approaches for specific needs can be obtained through the many resources drawn from material given in the Edgar Cayce readings during the 1877 - 1945 Cayce incarnation. Edgar Cayce and The Crystal Circle may be also contacted for updated and expanded information based on those readings, through trans-channel Laurel Steinhice, (615) 356-4280.
10. As our work together continues, we expect to provide several new or revised meditation/relaxation and self-realization techniques for possible publication and general use. As there are already many such resources that serve well, however, we will focus on other topics for the present.
11. It is this quality as an irritant of mucous membranes that often manifests as gastric distress after the ingestion of "spicy hot" foods. To minimize this distress and/or possible damage to the digestive system, one may take such remedies as Tagamet (by prescription), Maalox (non-prescription) or certain other similar substances without impairing the effectiveness of the spice's purifying action.
12. There is much additional information on internal cleansing

available through the A.R.E.'s materials drawn from the Cayce readings.

13. Extraterrestrial attachments are rare, though not unheard of.
14. Use of Christconsciousness or Christian terminology is more appropriate in some instances than in others, and it may be necessary to say the affirmation both ways to address the needs of various attaching entities. Some attachments are Christian in tradition; some are not! Whenever possible, we work closely with figures of the attachments' own faith during releases.
15. We don't suggest you adjust your body rhythms directly to "third dimensional vibrational frequency" because there are a wide variety of vibrational frequencies now personally interactive on the earth planet. They range from low third through intermediate and high third to low, intermediate and high fourth. You may already be in fourth - in which case you don't want to adjust back to third.

AFTERWORD

"Do you consider yourself to be enLightened?"

When someone asked me that question, I had to stop and think a moment, before I answered.

Am I enLightened?

Yes and No.

Compared to the person I was more than two decades ago, when I first entered into a career as a professional channel for The LightSource Group – we used to call it "The Crystal Circle", way back then – yes, I am definitely "enLightened".

I have learned so much, from the Guides of Universal Light who speak through me, among them the late great Edgar Cayce. I marvel at the information and insights they have shared with me, and with others through me. I am filled with the joyful Light of their loving and sustaining presence in my life, and with a deeper knowing of my own God-given spark of Light, within. I delight at being in a new, deeper, more complex harmony with the Earthplanet, and, as well, being on the cutting edge of new realities across the vastness of the cosmos.

Yes, compared to the person I once was, I am enLightened.

But... compared to the person I will be in another couple of decades, or another year or two, or even a few days from now? No, I am not yet enLightened. I am still a relatively uneducated seeker. And there is still so much more to learn!

Knowing Edgar Cayce, as a channel through whom he speaks, has been a wondrously educational experience for me – and I know there is more to come, as we walk together with our spiritual family of Light on the path toward eventual union with divine Oneness.

Yet looking back at how far we've come, in our journeys of understanding and exploration, I also feel great satisfaction in what we have accomplished thus far.

Edgar's "Tips" – the ones you have found in this little book – are timely ... and timeless. I encourage you to use them, to experiment with them, to build on them, and to enjoy them. I hope you will be inspired, as I am, to look forward to the lessons, the accomplishments – and the adventures! - that are still ahead of us.

Laurel Steinhice,
Trans-channel for The LightSource Group
Nashville, Tennessee, 2009

Watch for more books in The Rainbow Angels' Guide series from The LightSource Group, soon to come.

LaVergne, TN USA
29 September 2009
159334LV00001B/2/P

9 780980 168822